THE
PSYCHOLOGY
OF PROFIT

UNLOCKING BUSINESS SUCCESS

~GAURAV BAGHEL

COPYRIGHT

The Psychology of Profit: Unlocking Business Success

Printed in India

Cover design by: Gaurav Baghel

Interior design by: Gaurav Baghel

First Edition :2023

Gmail ID: mr.gaurav.baghel.official@gmail.com

DEDICATION

To my beloved family,

Throughout the journey of life, your unwavering support and boundless love have illuminated my path. In moments of doubt and triumph alike, you've been the steady anchor of my aspirations. Your belief in me, through thick and thin, has been the driving force behind the creation of this book.

With every page penned, I felt your presence, urging me forward. This book is not just a reflection of my efforts, but a testament to the strength of our familial bond.

With heartfelt gratitude, I dedicate this work to each of you, for your encouragement, sacrifices, and unwavering belief in my endeavors. Together, we have embarked on a remarkable journey, and I carry your love and support in every word.

With deepest love and appreciation,

-GAURAV BAGHEL

ACKNOWLEDGEMENT

 Writing this book has been a remarkable journey, one that I couldn't have embarked upon without the unwavering support and love of my family. To my parents, who instilled in me the values of perseverance and dedication, I am forever grateful.

A special acknowledgment goes to my mother, whose endless encouragement has been the driving force behind my endeavours. Your belief in me, your words of wisdom, and your unfaltering faith in my abilities have shaped me into the person I am today. Your strength and resilience have been my guiding light, and I dedicate this book to you with heartfelt appreciation.

I am fortunate to have an incredible family that has stood by me through every triumph and challenge. Your unwavering support has been my foundation, and I am blessed to have you in my corner. I extend my gratitude to my friends and mentors who provided valuable insights, feedback, and encouragement throughout this journey.

Your contributions have enriched this book and my understanding of the subject. Last but not least, I want to express my sincere appreciation to the readers. Your curiosity and interest in exploring the psychology of business have motivated me to create a work that I hope resonates with your aspirations.

As I conclude this journey, I carry with me the love and support that have illuminated my path. Thank you, from the bottom of my heart.

 With gratitude,

Gaurav Baghel

PREFACE

Welcome to "The Psychology of Profit: Unlocking Business Success." In a world where business landscapes are constantly evolving, understanding the intricate interplay between psychology and profitability is more essential than ever. This book is not just another business guide; it is a transformative exploration into the realms of human behaviour, decision-making, and the nuances that shape the path to success.

Amid the vast sea of business literature, this book sets itself apart by delving into the profound impact of psychology on profits. Beyond conventional strategies, we embark on a journey to uncover the hidden forces that drive consumer choices, influence leadership effectiveness, and shape organizational culture.

"The Psychology of Profits" is a culmination of insights drawn from the disciplines of psychology and business, offering a unique lens through which to view the dynamics of success. As you navigate these pages, you'll discover that this book isn't about formulaic solutions; it's about delving deep into the human psyche and uncovering the strategies that can propel your business toward sustained growth.

So, if you're ready to challenge your perceptions and embark on a journey of discovery, I invite you to immerse yourself in the pages that follow. "The Psychology of Profit" is your compass to navigate the intricate landscape of business success, where understanding the human mind becomes your most potent tool. Prepare to transcend conventional wisdom and embrace the extraordinary.

Let us unlock the potential that lies within the fusion of psychology and profits, and embark on a transformative voyage to lasting business success.

INTRODUCTION

Welcome to a journey that goes beyond balance sheets and profit margins. In "The Psychology of Profit: Unlocking Business Success," we delve into the intricate interplay between human behaviour, decision-making, and the bottom line. This isn't just another business book; it's a revelation that unveils the hidden dimensions of success.

In a world driven by consumer choices and market dynamics, understanding the psychology behind profits is paramount.

We embark on a voyage that explores the underlying forces shaping consumer preferences, the impact of leadership styles, and the art of fostering a thriving organizational culture.

This book isn't about mere tactics; it's about gaining Insights into the minds of consumers, employees, and leaders. By blending psychology and business principles, we empower you to navigate the complexities of the modern business landscape with confidence.

Through real-world examples, actionable strategies, and thought-provoking insights, "The Psychology of Profit" equips you with the tools to make informed decisions, foster innovation, and cultivate a prosperous business environment.

Prepare to embark on a journey that transforms your perspective on profitability. Let's unravel the psychology behind profits and navigate the path to enduring success.

CONTENT

GIFTED SECTIONS

Chapter: 1

The Psychology of Prosperity

Unlocking the Mindset for Abundant Success

Embarking on the Profitable Journey

In a world where fortunes can change in an instant and the pursuit of wealth is a universal aspiration, there's a remarkable aspect often overlooked—the way our minds shape our financial destinies. Imagine stepping into this fascinating realm where profit isn't just about numbers, but about the hidden workings of our thoughts and behaviors. In this very first chapter, we're embarking on a journey to unravel the mysteries of the "Psychology of Prosperity." Think of it as laying the foundation for a profound exploration of what drives us toward financial success, both individually and in business.

Here, we'll begin to uncover the secrets, understand the truths, and tap into the untapped potential that can turn profit-making into a path to lasting prosperity. So, get ready for a transformative adventure, where the first impression is the key to unlocking a world of financial triumph.

Now, let's shift our focus to the very first topic at hand—the "Profitable Mindset."

The Profitable Mindset

In a world where fortunes can change in the blink of an eye, and the pursuit of wealth resonates as a universal aspiration, there exists a facet of this relentless quest that often remains shrouded in the shadows—the profound influence of our minds on the shaping of our financial destinies. Within these pages, you are invited to embark on a profound journey, one that transcends the mere arithmetic of profit and instead seeks to unravel the intricate tapestry of the "Psychology of Prosperity."

In this inaugural chapter, we lay the cornerstone for an exploration that transcends superficial notions, a voyage that delves deep into the very essence of what propels individuals and enterprises toward the pinnacles of financial success. It is here that we begin to unfurl the enigma that is the "Profitable Mindset," a formidable asset in our pursuit of lasting prosperity.

The Psychology of Abundance:

Picture, if you will, two entrepreneurs encountering a similar setback along their respective journeys. One, blessed with an abundance mindset, sees this momentary challenge not as an insurmountable obstacle but as an opportunity—an opportunity to innovate, to adapt, and ultimately, to thrive. The other, ensnared by a scarcity mindset, perceives the same challenge as a harbinger of doom, a roadblock with no conceivable detour. It is within the realm of the abundance mindset that creativity blossoms, resilience thrives, and the audacity to explore uncharted avenues of profit takes root.

Goal Setting for Profit:

Setting financial goals is akin to charting a course across uncharted waters; it is the compass that guides our actions, the North Star illuminating the path to profit. Effective goal setting, however, is not a mere exercise in wishful thinking; it is a strategic endeavor governed by the following principles:

1.Specificity: Herein lies the importance of clarity; our financial objectives must be meticulously defined, transcending vague aspirations like "make more money" and instead adopting concrete targets, complete with quantifiable metrics and timelines.

2.Measurability: Goals are most potent when they are measurable, rendering the progress tangible and facilitating informed adjustments to our strategies.

3.Realism: Though ambition is commendable, the goals we set must be attainable through concerted effort and commitment. Goals that soar into the stratosphere of unattainability serve only to breed frustration.

4.Relevance: The alignment of these objectives with our overarching vision and values is paramount. Goals with intrinsic meaning are the most potent motivators.

Imagine these goals as waypoints on your expedition—a destination, a checkpoint, a milestone.

Certainly, let's transition seamlessly from this topic to a deep dive into "Self-Belief and Confidence,"

Self-Belief and Confidence:

Confidence, akin to the wind filling our sails, serves as the driving force behind our relentless pursuit of profit. It is a quality not characterized by the absence of self-doubt, but rather by the audacity to act resolutely despite its presence. Cultivating confidence is a multifaceted and intricate endeavor, one that requires careful nurturing through various means:

A continuous and positive inner dialogue plays a pivotal role. It involves a ceaseless conversation with our inner selves, where self-doubt is replaced by a cascade of affirmations and positive narratives that celebrate our inherent abilities. This dialogue is the fertile soil from which confidence sprouts and thrives.

Visualization, the act of mentally envisaging our own success, stands as another potent tool in our arsenal. It empowers us to traverse the most daunting obstacles with unwavering self-assurance. By painting vivid mental images of our achievements, we not only bolster our belief in ourselves but also pave the path to making those visions a reality.

Furthermore, the presence of mentors and a robust support network acts as the bedrock upon which our self-belief can flourish.

These individuals provide us with guidance, wisdom, and unwavering encouragement. In times of turbulence, they offer the fortitude required to weather storms, helping us navigate through uncertainty with newfound confidence.

In essence, confidence is the cornerstone of our profitable journey. It is not a static trait but a dynamic force that can be nurtured and fortified, leading us towards greater financial success.

Now, let's pivot our attention from the current discourse to a subject of paramount significance—mastering the relentless battle against the daunting specter of failure.

Overcoming the Fear of Failure:

Fear of failure, a pervasive barrier to profitable thinking, can often paralyze individuals, deterring them from undertaking the essential risks that accompany entrepreneurial endeavors. To surmount this fear, consider the following strategies:

Embrace a Growth Mindset: Redefine failure not as a terminus, but as a transformative stepping stone on the path to growth and enlightenment. Break your Goals into Smaller Steps Divide towering ambitions into manageable, bite-sized tasks, rendering them less daunting and diminishing the trepidation tied to potential setbacks. **Learn from Failure Stories:** Study the sagas of prosperous entrepreneurs who traversed the valleys of failure before scaling the peaks of success. These narratives underscore that failure is not a deviation from the path, but an integral part of the journey. By delving deep into these psychological facets, we endeavor to construct a mindset conducive to profitable thinking and entrepreneurial triumph. This mindset equips us to confront challenges with grace, to articulate and pursue financial ambitions, and to act with unshakable confidence.

Now, with our exploration of the "Profitable Mindset" behind us, let us pivot our focus to a profound subject—a journey into the intricate relationship between "Money and Motivation." In traversing these uncharted waters of the psyche, you are not merely a passenger; you are the captain of your destiny, charting a course towards the shores of lasting prosperity.

Money and Motivation

Understanding the psychology of money is an indispensable cornerstone of achieving financial success. Money wields profound influence over our behavior and decision-making, serving both as a potent motivator and a potential source of stress. At its core, this comprehension hinges on several key facets.

Financial stress, a ubiquitous concern, often takes root in circumstances such as financial insecurity, debt burdens, or uncontrolled expenditures. Recognizing the origins of financial stress is paramount, as it empowers individuals to address these challenges, fostering a clear and profit-oriented mindset.

Another crucial aspect entails examining one's financial habits and behaviors. This introspective exploration represents the initial stride toward enhancing financial self-mastery. Understanding whether one is inclined toward spending or saving, and whether investments are made judiciously, paves the way for necessary adjustments in pursuit of profitability. Moreover, discerning the triggers that prompt specific financial behaviors unlocks the potential for conscious decision-making. For instance, emotional spending frequently emerges in response to stress or boredom. Identifying these triggers provides the ability to mitigate their impact and make more financially astute choices.

Intrinsic vs. Extrinsic Motivation

Profitable thinking aligns motivation with business objectives, distinguishing between two primary motivational paradigms: intrinsic and extrinsic.

Intrinsic motivation derives from inner satisfaction and personal fulfillment, often intertwining with the joy found in the work itself. Its distinctive quality lies in sustainability, as it isn't contingent solely upon external rewards.

Conversely, **extrinsic motivation** hinges upon external factors such as monetary gain, fame, or recognition. While these external stimuli can ignite initial motivation, they may prove insufficient for long-term commitment and may even precipitate burnout if rewards aren't consistently met.

For profit-minded individuals, achieving balance between intrinsic and extrinsic motivations is paramount. This equilibrium may manifest as personal gratification drawn from their work, harmoniously supplemented by the recognition of the significance of financial rewards in supporting their objectives.

Crafting motivational goals attuned to one's intrinsic and extrinsic drivers becomes pivotal. This alignment ensures that each goal resonates with individual motivations, such as deriving satisfaction from aiding others or creating products and services that enrich lives.

Financial Vision

Finally, crafting a compelling financial vision serves as the North Star on the journey to profitability. This vision comprises several integral elements.

Clarity lies at the heart of a robust financial vision—it must be well-defined and transparent. Such clarity not only guides one's financial decisions but also underscores the path toward achieving them.

Motivation represents another crucial facet. A potent financial vision should ignite excitement and ardor, galvanizing individuals to pursue their financial goals unwaveringly, even in the face of adversity. Alignment with personal values and long-term objectives is essential. When a financial vision reflects what truly matters, it transforms into a formidable force propelling one toward profit.

Lastly, a financial vision should exhibit adaptability, remaining open to evolution as one progresses on their journey. This dynamism ensures relevance and resilience in the ever-changing landscape of financial endeavors.

In essence, comprehending the psychology of money, cultivating motivation, and nurturing a compelling financial vision form the bedrock of profitable thinking and financial triumph.

Now, let's redirect our focus to a captivating subject—delving into the intricate concept of 'Delayed Gratification.

Delayed Gratification:

Profitable thinking often involves delaying immediate rewards for long-term gains. Key points to consider:

1.Short-Term Sacrifices: Delayed gratification may require making short-term sacrifices, such as reinvesting profits back into the business or saving rather than spending.

2.Long-Term Perspective: Adopting a long-term perspective helps you prioritize future financial security and prosperity over immediate pleasures.

3.Resisting Temptation: It's essential to resist the temptation of instant gratification, which can lead to impulsive financial decisions.

4.Building Discipline: Developing discipline is key to embracing delayed gratification. Creating habits that support your long-term goals is a worthwhile investment in profit.

By understanding the complex interplay between money and motivation, including the psychology of money, intrinsic and extrinsic motivation, financial vision, and delayed gratification, individuals can cultivate a mindset that's conducive to profitable thinking and financial success. These insights will empower them to make informed financial decisions, stay motivated, and pursue their profit-oriented goals effectively.

The Power of Perception

In the world of business, perception stands as a linchpin upon which decisions are hinged, opportunities are recognized, and success is ultimately shaped. It encompasses how individuals interpret and make sense of the ever-evolving business landscape, influencing the very essence of entrepreneurial endeavors.

1.The Perceptual Landscape: At its core, perception in business embodies how individuals view and understand the world around them. It is a multifaceted lens through which the myriad facets of the business realm come into focus.

2.Opportunity and Challenge: Perception plays a pivotal role in identifying opportunities and addressing challenges. A growth mindset, intertwined with one's perception, often leads to the astute recognition of opportunities and an agile approach to surmounting challenges. In this light, what some might view as insurmountable obstacles are seen as fertile ground for innovation and profit by others.

3.Strategic Vision: Accurate perception of the competitive landscape and market dynamics is foundational for crafting effective business strategies. A nuanced understanding of market conditions informs strategic planning, positioning, and the ability to maintain a competitive edge.

4.Risk Assessment: Perception extends to how risks associated with business decisions are evaluated. The lens through which individuals perceive these risks significantly influences their willingness to embark on calculated ventures. Consequently, an informed grasp of risk perception becomes instrumental in fostering prudent risk management practices.

5.Market Awareness: Perception is equally germane to recognizing and interpreting market trends. These trends, when perceptively discerned, serve as harbingers of profitable strategies. Adapting offerings and strategies in alignment with emerging consumer behavior or market shifts can lead to sustained profitability.

6.Leveraging Positive Framing: Strategic positive framing, a potent tool across various business domains, involves presenting information and situations in a favorable light. This artful presentation enhances customer perception, instills confidence in investors, motivates employees, and facilitates adept crisis management.

7.Embracing Change: A dynamic perception of change as a wellspring of innovation and growth is central to profit-oriented thinking. In the face of evolving market dynamics and consumer expectations, businesses that perceive change as an opportunity are better equipped to adapt their strategies and offerings, staying agile, competitive, and ultimately, profitable.

In essence, perception in business is the fulcrum upon which a multitude of pivotal decisions and actions pivot. It is the discerning eye that identifies opportunities in challenges, formulates effective strategies, evaluates risks, harnesses the power of cognitive biases, employs positive framing, and views change as a catalyst for innovation and growth. Understanding and harnessing the power of perception is not just a business skill; it is the cornerstone of profitable thinking and the psychology of profit itself.

Turning Challenges into Triumphs: Real-Life Inspiration:

In the world of business, few stories resonate as powerfully as that of Steve Jobs, the visionary co-founder of Apple Inc. His journey is a testament to the profound impact of a profitable mindset, effective goal-setting, self-belief, and the ability to embrace change—all themes we've explored in this chapter.

Steve Jobs possessed an unwavering belief in his vision. He envisioned a world where personal computers were not just tools but seamless extensions of our lives. Jobs' confidence in his ideas was unshakeable, even In the face of setbacks.

One of his most iconic moments was his return to Apple in 1997 when the company was on the brink of bankruptcy. At this critical juncture, he made a daring decision—to drastically simplify the product lineup, focus on core offerings, and innovate relentlessly. His ability to embrace change and pivot the company's direction toward a more streamlined and innovative approach paid off handsomely.

He was known for his attention to detail and perfectionism, qualities rooted in a profitable mindset. He understood the importance of creating products that weren't just functional but beautifully designed. His emphasis on user experience and design aesthetics revolutionized the tech industry, setting Apple apart from its competitors. The concept of delayed gratification was also central to

Jobs' success. Instead of rushing products to market, he was willing to delay releases until they met his exacting standards. This approach, while frustrating to some, ensured that Apple's products were consistently top-notch, commanding premium prices and customer loyalty. His ability to perceive market trends and consumer desires was another key factor. He recognized the potential of the iPod, iPhone, and iPad long before these products became mainstream. His visionary perception enabled Apple to lead in these product categories, reaping enormous profits.

Throughout his career, Steve Jobs epitomized the power of perception in business. He saw opportunities where others saw obstacles, embraced change as a source of innovation, and understood the value of delayed gratification. His story serves as an inspiring example of how implementing these strategies can lead not only to financial success but also to a lasting legacy of innovation and transformation in the business world. As you continue reading, keep Jobs' journey in mind, and let it inspire your own profitable mindset and path to prosperity.

Chapter 2:

The Psychology of Financial Success

Mastering Money, Mastering Life

Unraveling the Mindset of Financial Success

In this pivotal chapter, we embark on a transformative journey into the web of financial psychology, a realm where our beliefs, attitudes, and choices converge to shape our financial destinies. Money, often regarded as the cornerstone of our lives, is not merely a means of exchange but a reflection of our deepest convictions. Welcome to 'The Psychology of Financial Success,' where we unravel the mysteries of mastering money, transcending limitations, and cultivating a mindset that paves the way for a prosperous future. As we delve deeper into the chapters of this book, you'll discover that financial success is not solely about numbers on a balance sheet; it's a harmonious interplay between our thoughts, actions, and aspirations. Join us on this enlightening exploration as we uncover the profound impact of your money beliefs, the art of setting SMART financial goals, understanding your risk tolerance, and making informed investment decisions. This chapter marks the beginning of a remarkable journey towards financial empowerment, where you'll learn to master money and, in turn, master life itself.

Money Beliefs and Attitudes

The impact of childhood money messages is a testament to the enduring influence of our early environment. These messages, imprinted in our minds during our formative years, create the lens through which we perceive and engage with financial opportunities. They shape our financial identity, guiding our choices, and often operating beneath our conscious awareness. In understanding this dynamic, we gain the power to rewrite these scripts and reshape our financial destiny. Identifying limiting beliefs requires a willingness to confront our own perceived shortcomings and self-imposed constraints. These beliefs, often deeply ingrained, act as barriers that hold us back from embracing our full financial potential. However, the act of recognition and the subsequent commitment to challenge and overcome these limitations are profound acts of self-empowerment. It is through this process that we unlock new avenues for financial growth and prosperity. Cultivating a positive money mindset is akin to tending to the soil in which our financial goals take root. It involves nurturing a mindset that views money as a tool of empowerment rather than a source of anxiety or constraint. With this mindset, we approach financial decisions with confidence, unafraid to take calculated risks, and explore opportunities that align with our aspirations. A positive money mindset empowers us to set ambitious yet achievable financial goals, paving the way for a future defined by financial abundance and security.

In essence, the journey into the psychology of financial success is a transformative voyage that transcends mere fiscal matters. It is a profound exploration of the human psyche and its intricate relationship with money. By acknowledging the Impact of childhood messages, identifying and dismantling limiting beliefs, and cultivating a positive money mindset, we equip ourselves with the tools to navigate the complex terrain of financial success. This chapter marks the beginning of an enlightening expedition towards financial empowerment—a journey where we master money and, in turn, master life itself.

Now in this chapter, we shift our focus to the precision of setting S.M.A.R.T. financial objectives, where intentions evolve into concrete milestones on your journey to financial success."

S.M.A.R.T. Financial Goals:

Setting financial goals is an art that transforms aspirations into actionable plans. The acronym S.M.A.R.T. stands for Specific,

Measurable, Achievable, Relevant, and Time-bound. It's a strategic framework that brings precision and clarity to your financial objectives, ensuring they are well-crafted and effective in guiding your path to success.

Specific: Specificity is the cornerstone of effective goal setting. Rather than vague aspirations like "I want to save money," a specific goal is sharply defined. For example, "I want to save $10,000 for a down payment on a house within three years" provides a clear target. Specific goals offer clarity and direction, eliminating ambiguity and setting a precise destination for your financial journey.

Measurable: Measurability is essential to gauge your progress over time. It means having a quantifiable metric to track your success. In our example, measuring progress is as simple as regularly checking your savings account balance. This tracking mechanism ensures you're on course and allows for adjustments if needed. Measurable goals prevent you from getting lost in the nebulous realm of wishful thinking.

Achievable: While ambition is admirable, setting realistic and attainable goals is crucial. Goals should be challenging yet within reach with effort and dedication. Setting goals that are too far-fetched can lead to frustration and demotivation. Achievable goals acknowledge your current resources and capabilities while inspiring you to strive for excellence.

Relevant: Relevance ties your financial goals to your broader life objectives. They should align with your values, long-term vision, and overall aspirations. Each goal should have a meaningful place within the grand scheme of your life. Relevant goals ensure that your financial pursuits are purposeful and contribute to your holistic well-being.

Time-bound: Goals need a deadline to create a sense of urgency and commitment. Without a timeframe, there's a lack of motivation to work diligently toward your objectives. In our example, the three-year deadline for saving $10,000 for a house down payment provides a clear time-bound element. It prompts action and ensures you stay on track.

In essence, S.M.A.R.T. financial goals are the compass that guides your financial journey. They transform vague desires into well-structured, achievable milestones. By adhering to these principles, you pave the way for a future where your financial dreams become tangible realities, and your journey to financial success is marked by purpose, clarity, and measurable progress.

Prepare to be spellbound by 'The Power of Compound Interest,' a financial enchantment that transforms small investments into a cascade of wealth. In this captivating journey, we'll unveil the sorcery behind exponential financial growth, where your dollars work their magic and your financial future sparkles with promise.

The Power of Compound Interest:

Compound Interest, a financial powerhouse, possesses the potential to significantly amplify your wealth as it accrues not just on your initial investment, but also on previously earned interest. Imagine this: you invest $1,000 at an annual interest rate of 5%, resulting in $50 of interest in the first year. In the second year, your earnings extend beyond the original $1,000, encompassing the $50 interest from the previous year. This compounding effect perpetuates, turbocharging your returns. The key to harnessing this financial wizardry lies in initiating investments early and maintaining consistency. The longer your money compounds, the greater your potential for substantial wealth accumulation.

Understanding and implementing strategies such as setting specific, measurable, achievable, relevant, and time-bound (S.M.A.R.T.) financial goals, crafting a budget and savings plan, exploring investment avenues that align with your objectives and risk tolerance, and unlocking the power of compound interest are the essential tools in your arsenal for financial success. These strategies not only propel you toward your financial objectives but also ensure a more secure and prosperous future.

"Financial institutions often provide risk assessment questionnaires, meticulously designed to assess your willingness to embrace various levels of investment risk. Your age, financial objectives, and investment horizon all factor into this assessment. However, personal reflection plays an equally crucial role. It involves an honest examination of your feelings and reactions towards financial risk. Are you willing to accept the possibility of loss in exchange for the potential of higher returns, or do you lean towards the stability of conservative, lower-risk investments? Your risk tolerance is a dynamic element that also influences your diversification strategy. Conservative investors tend to gravitate towards safer assets such as bonds, prioritizing wealth preservation. In contrast, more daring investors may willingly embrace riskier, albeit potentially more lucrative, investments like stocks, aiming for greater wealth accumulation. Recognizing the nuanced interplay of risk tolerance is a key asset in aligning your investment choices with your financial objectives. This comprehension extends to acknowledging that your tolerance may vary between short-term and long-term goals, allowing for a more precise allocation of assets that suits each distinct horizon.

Financial institutions offer risk assessment questionnaires, finely tuned instruments designed to probe your willingness to embrace the spectrum of investment risk. These questionnaires carefully consider your age, financial objectives, and investment timeline, offering a comprehensive evaluation. Yet, the subjective dimension of personal reflection remains equally crucial. It beckons you to engage in introspection, delving into your emotions and reactions concerning financial risk. Are you prepared to face the possibility of loss in exchange for the tantalizing prospects of higher returns, or do you gravitate towards the stability of more conservative, lower-risk investments? Risk tolerance, a dynamic facet of your financial persona, also exerts its influence on your diversification strategy. Conservative investors often gravitate towards safer havens like bonds, prioritizing the preservation of wealth. Conversely, audacious investors may embrace riskier yet potentially more rewarding avenues, such as stocks, with the aim of accumulating greater wealth.

Acknowledging this intricate interplay of risk tolerance extends to recognizing that your tolerance levels may fluctuate between short-term and long-term financial goals. This awareness empowers you to sculpt a meticulous allocation of assets that harmonizes with each distinctive horizon.

With these insights into the intricacies of risk tolerance and a fortified understanding of the power of compound interest, your journey in the financial decision-making becomes a confident stride towards an enriched and secure financial future. The fusion of knowledge and strategy positions you as a master of your financial destiny, poised to navigate the multifaceted terrain of wealth creation and preservation.

Turning Challenges into Triumphs: Real-Life Inspiration:

Let's explore the remarkable journey of Warren Buffett, a man known as one of the most successful investors of all time. Buffett, often referred to as the 'Oracle of Omaha,' was born in 1930 in

Omaha, Nebraska, into a family with a strong business and investment background. From a young age, Buffett displayed a keen interest in finance and investing. He began his entrepreneurial ventures early, from selling gum to delivering newspapers. By the age of 11, he had already made his first investment in the stock market. His early experiences instilled in him the value of money and the importance of making sound financial decisions.

Buffett's success story is deeply intertwined with the principles we've explored in this chapter. He is renowned for his ability to set S.M.A.R.T. financial goals and stick to them rigorously. His ultimate goal was to build wealth through prudent investing, and he did just that. He set specific targets for the companies he invested in, focusing on their intrinsic value and long-term potential.

The power of compound interest played a pivotal role in Buffett's wealth accumulation. He started investing early in life and continued to do so consistently. This strategy allowed him to benefit from the compounding effect, where his returns generated more returns over time. He once famously remarked that his wealth really took off when he was in his 40s, emphasizing the importance of patience and long-term thinking. Warren Buffett's approach to risk was calculated and disciplined. He never invested in businesses he didn't understand and always had a margin of safety to protect his investments. This careful risk management, combined with his deep knowledge of businesses, contributed to his remarkable success.

Over the years, Buffett's investments in companies like Coca-Cola, Apple, and Berkshire Hathaway have grown exponentially. His wealth has made him one of the richest people globally, yet he remains known for his frugal lifestyle and commitment to philanthropy.

Warren Buffett's investment philosophy is often summarized in the phrase "value investing." He believed in buying undervalued companies with strong fundamentals and holding onto them for the long term. This patient approach allowed him to weather market fluctuations and benefit from the compounding of his investments.

One of the key takeaways from Buffett's success is the importance of continuous learning. Throughout his life, he voraciously read and studied financial reports, business models, and economic trends. He was known for his intellectual curiosity and willingness to adapt his investment strategies based on new information. Buffett also emphasized the significance of ethics and integrity in business dealings. He famously said, "It takes 20 years to build a reputation and five minutes to ruin it. If you think about that, you'll do things differently." This commitment to ethical behavior and transparency not only earned him respect but also solidified his reputation as a trustworthy and reliable investor. While Warren Buffett's financial achievements are indeed awe-inspiring, his humility and down-to-earth demeanor make him an even more compelling figure. He lives a relatively modest lifestyle, famously residing in the same Omaha home he purchased in 1958. His frugality and lack of ostentation serve as a powerful reminder that financial success doesn't require extravagance but rather sound financial principles.

Warren Buffett's journey to financial success is a testament to the principles discussed in this chapter. He understood the importance of mastering, setting clear financial goals, harnessing the power of compound interest, and managing risk effectively. His life story serves as a compelling reminder that anyone, with dedication and adherence to sound financial principles, can master money, build wealth, and leave a lasting legacy of their own.

Chapter 3:

The Psychology of Profitable Thinking

Where Thoughts Turn into Wealth

Unlocking the Mind's Fortune

In the vast domain of finance, the mind assumes a dual role—both architect and alchemist—forging abstract ideas into concrete fortunes and molding dreams into tangible wealth. This chapter delves into the intricate realm of the "Psychology of Profitable Thinking." Here, cognition becomes a form of currency, not just a theoretical concept but a boundless source of prosperity. In this intellectual journey, we will unveil the transformation of thoughts into assets, ideas into a potent arsenal for financial success. From understanding perception's influence to mastering delayed gratification, this chapter serves as your roadmap in the voyage where thoughts hold value, and the mind, the mint.

Shift your focus to tangible wealth creation. Uncover strategies to turn your thoughts into income-generating actions. Explore the realms of opportunity recognition, delayed gratification, and the alchemy of wealth through the mind. Embark on a journey towards financial abundance.

Income Generation

In the pursuit of financial prosperity, the art of generating income stands as a cornerstone. Let's delves into the multifaceted strategies and mindsets behind income generation, exploring the diverse avenues through which individuals and businesses can cultivate a steady stream of wealth. From entrepreneurial ventures to investment insights, we uncover the secrets to not only making money but also nurturing and growing it. Get ready to embark on a journey through the world of "Income Generation," where financial success is not just a destination but a continuous, profit-driven voyage.

Diverse Income Streams: The Foundation of Financial Security

In the pursuit of financial success, embracing the concept of diverse income streams becomes a strategic imperative. This multifaceted approach to income generation yields several compelling advantages, each deserving of its own spotlight:

1. Financial Stability:

Relying solely on a single income source can render an individual financially vulnerable in the face of life's uncertainties. Unexpected challenges, such as job loss or economic downturns, can have a profound impact on one's financial well-being when the entirety of income originates from a solitary channel. In contrast, diversification acts as a sturdy safety net. When unforeseen circumstances strike, having multiple income streams ensures that the impact on overall finances is cushioned. It's akin to spreading your financial risk across various avenues, reducing the chances of catastrophic setbacks. This sense of security not only shields you from turmoil but also bolsters your overall financial resilience.

2. Multiple Opportunities:

The pursuit of diverse income streams isn't merely a risk mitigation strategy; it's an invitation to explore a multitude of opportunities. Beyond the primary job or income source, diversification opens doors to various income-generating ventures. These can manifest as side businesses, freelance work, or investments in endeavors that have the potential to bolster your earnings. Embracing these supplementary streams of income isn't solely about protecting your financial stability; it's about unlocking growth potential. Each additional income source contributes not only to your financial security but also to your capacity for financial growth. It's akin to cultivating multiple crops in your financial garden, ensuring a bountiful harvest of financial rewards.

3. Enhanced Savings and Investments:

Diverse income streams offer more than immediate financial stability and growth opportunities; they also serve as a wellspring of surplus funds. These additional funds, beyond meeting your day-to-day expenses, can be channeled toward savings and investments. This surplus capital turbocharges your wealth-building endeavors. Instead of merely earning a paycheck, you are essentially multiplying your financial potential. By allocating these surplus earnings wisely into savings accounts, investment portfolios, or other wealth-building vehicles, you set yourself on an accelerated trajectory toward financial prosperity. Diversification isn't just about earning more; it's about optimizing the use of your earnings to create a more secure and prosperous future.

In essence, the concept of diverse income streams isn't confined to financial jargon; it's the very foundation upon which financial security and success are built. It offers protection against unforeseen financial turbulence, encourages exploration of new income-generating avenues, and supercharges your ability to save and invest, ultimately paving the path to enduring financial well-being.

Shifting our focus from income generation, let's dive into the dynamic realm of Career Advancement: Fueling Your Primary Income Source. This chapter will equip you with the strategies and insights to propel your career forward, ensuring that your primary income remains strong and fulfilling. Prepare to unlock the keys to professional success and advancement.

Career Advancement: Fueling Your Primary Income Source

In the journey toward financial success, your career serves as the primary income source, representing a significant portion of your financial prosperity. To fully harness its potential, consider the following strategies:

1. Skill Development: The Art of Continuous Improvement

Your career is a dynamic landscape that thrives on innovation and adaptability. To excel and ascend the ranks, it's essential to commit to ongoing skill development and knowledge enhancement. Continuously updating and upgrading your skill set ensures that you remain at the forefront of your field. This proactive approach not only makes you an invaluable asset to your organization but also opens doors to lucrative opportunities. Embrace professional development opportunities, attend workshops, earn certifications, and stay attuned to industry trends. By doing so, you position yourself as a high-achieving professional with the ability to tackle new challenges and responsibilities.

2. Networking: Building Bridges to Opportunity

The power of a robust professional network cannot be overstated. Your network acts as a gateway to new job opportunities, mentorship relationships, and collaborations that can propel your career to new heights. Invest time in nurturing and expanding your network, both within and outside your organization. Attend industry events, engage in online forums and communities, and seek out mentorship from seasoned professionals. These connections can provide valuable insights, offer guidance during critical career junctures, and even lead to collaborations that augment your income. Remember, in the arena of career advancement, it's often not just what you know but who you know that can make all the difference.

3. Negotiation Skills: Advocating for Your Worth

Effective negotiation is a skill that can significantly impact your income trajectory. Many professionals underestimate the power of negotiation in their careers. Whether you're negotiating a starting salary, requesting a raise, or advocating for better benefits, honing your negotiation skills is crucial. It's an opportunity to assert your worth and secure financial gains that accumulate over time. Don't shy away from negotiating for what you deserve. Research industry standards, prepare a compelling case for your request, and approach negotiations with confidence. Over the course of your career, these negotiation victories can translate into substantial income increases, ultimately contributing to your financial success.

As you navigate the domain of career advancement, remember that your primary income source is not static; it's a dynamic force that can be optimized through skill development, networking, and effective negotiation. Your commitment to these strategies positions you for long-term financial prosperity by ensuring that your career remains a robust foundation for your financial success.

Investment Vehicles

Diverse Investment Options: Real estate is just one piece of the investment puzzle. Numerous investment vehicles are available, each with its own risk-reward profile. A well-rounded investment portfolio should encompass various vehicles, each offering its unique risk-reward profile. Let's delve into these diverse investment options and explore the array of opportunities available to investors:

1.Stocks: The Engines of Corporate Ownership

When you invest in stocks, you're essentially buying shares of ownership in publicly traded companies. This means you become a shareholder in these companies and have a stake in their success. Stocks have the potential to provide significant returns on your investment over the long term, making them an attractive choice for many investors. However, it's important to note that stocks are also associated with higher volatility. This means that their prices can fluctuate significantly in the short term due to various factors such as economic conditions, market sentiment, or company-specific news. These fluctuations can lead to both gains and losses in your investment portfolio. To manage the risk associated with investing in stocks, diversification is a key strategy. Diversifying your stock portfolio involves spreading your investments across different industries and sectors. By doing so, you reduce the impact of poor performance in a specific sector on your overall portfolio.

For example, if one industry experiences a downturn, the positive performance of stocks in other industries can help offset those losses.

2.Bonds: The Foundation of Fixed Income

Bonds are debt securities issued by governments, municipalities, or corporations to raise capital. When you invest in bonds, you essentially become a lender, providing the issuer with a loan in exchange for periodic interest payments and the return of the bond's face value at maturity. Bonds are generally considered lower-risk investments compared to stocks. They offer a fixed income stream through regular interest payments, which can be attractive to income-focused investors. This regular income can provide financial stability and is often used for capital preservation. The risk associated with bonds primarily relates to the issuer's creditworthiness. In other words, there's a risk that the issuer may default on its interest payments or fail to repay the bond's face value at maturity.

To mitigate this risk, investors often seek bonds from reputable issuers with strong credit ratings. Bonds also have an inverse relationship with interest rates. When interest rates rise, bond prices tend to fall, and vice versa. This interest rate risk can impact the value of your bond investments, particularly if you need to sell them before maturity.

3.Mutual Funds and ETFs: The Power of Diversification

Mutual funds and exchange-traded funds (ETFs) are investment vehicles that pool money from multiple investors to create a diversified portfolio of assets, which can include stocks, bonds, or other securities. These investment options offer several advantages:

- Diversification: One of the key benefits of mutual funds and ETFs is diversification. By investing in these vehicles, you gain exposure to a wide range of securities, reducing the risk associated with individual stock or bond picking. Diversification can help spread risk and potentially improve overall portfolio performance.
- Professional Management: Mutual funds and many ETFs are managed by professional fund managers who make investment decisions on behalf of investors. This expertise can be valuable, especially for those who may not have the time or knowledge to manage their investments actively.
- Liquidity: Mutual funds and ETFs are typically highly liquid, meaning you can buy and sell shares on most business days at the fund's net asset value (NAV). This liquidity provides flexibility and access to your investment capital when needed.

It's important to note that mutual funds and ETFs come in various types, each with its own investment strategy and objectives. Some funds focus on specific asset classes, such as equity (stock) funds, bond funds, or real estate funds, while others may target particular sectors or industries. Additionally, mutual funds can be actively managed, where fund managers actively select and manage the fund's investments, or passively managed, with their performance tracking a specific index. ETFs, on the other hand, are often passively managed and aim to replicate the performance of a specific index.

While mutual funds and ETFs offer diversification and professional management, they are not entirely risk-free. Like all investments, they can be subject to market fluctuations and carry their own set of risks. Understanding the specific objectives, fees, and risks associated with a particular fund is essential before investing.

Risk Management

In the world of wealth creation, prudent risk management is your guiding light. Picture it as the compass that keeps your financial journey on course, ensuring you reach your destination unscathed. This chapter is your roadmap to understanding, evaluating, and ultimately mitigating the myriad risks that can threaten your financial well-being. From navigating market turbulence to securing your investments, we'll explore strategies and principles that empower you to safeguard your financial future. So, fasten your seatbelts; we're embarking on a journey were foresight and strategy reign supreme.

Risk Assessment: Understanding Your Comfort Zone

At the core of successful investing lies the essential task of risk assessment. This process entails a deep dive into your personal relationship with risk and serves as the cornerstone of your investment strategy. Imagine risk as a vast ocean with waters ranging from tranquil to turbulent. Your approach to this ocean is unique and influenced by various factors that make up your financial profile. These factors include:

Financial Objectives: Start by defining your financial goals. Are you saving for retirement, planning to purchase a home, or aiming to fund your child's education? Each objective comes with its timeline and funding requirements, shaping the level of risk you can afford.

Investment Horizon: Your investment horizon represents the length of time you plan to hold an investment before needing to access the funds. For instance, retirement savings may have a long investment horizon, allowing for a more extended period to ride out market fluctuations, while short-term goals like buying a car may require a more conservative approach.

Emotional Resilience: Understanding how you react to market volatility is crucial. Are you comfortable with the idea of your investments experiencing temporary declines, or does the thought of market turbulence keep you awake at night? Emotional resilience is a fundamental aspect of risk tolerance.

Once you've contemplated these factors, you'll have a clearer picture of your comfort zone within the risk spectrum. This zone is where you feel secure and confident in your investment decisions, and it's unique to you. Some individuals may find themselves comfortable with higher levels of risk, seeking potentially higher returns. Others may prefer a more conservative approach to preserve capital and minimize volatility.

The introspection you've undertaken in this risk assessment forms the bedrock of your investment strategy. It's not just about numbers; it's about aligning your investments with your financial aspirations and emotional well-being. Armed with this understanding, you can tailor your portfolio to reflect your risk tolerance, ensuring a smoother and more successful investment journey.

Diversification

Diversification is a fundamental risk management strategy in investing. It involves spreading your investments across a variety of different asset classes and securities to reduce the impact that any one poorly performing asset can have on your overall portfolio.

Imagine you have a portfolio consisting solely of stocks from a single industry. If that industry experiences a downturn, your entire portfolio could suffer significant losses. However, if you diversify by including stocks from different industries, bonds, and perhaps other asset types like real estate or commodities, you are less exposed to the risk of a single sector's downturn affecting your entire portfolio.

Diversification can be achieved in several ways. You can use mutual funds or exchange-traded funds (ETFs), which pool money from multiple investors to create diversified portfolios automatically. Alternatively, you can individually select a mix of asset types in your portfolio. The key takeaway is that diversification helps spread risk, making your investment portfolio more resilient to market fluctuations and potentially improving your overall returns.

Diversification is like the adage "Don't put all your eggs in one basket" applied to investing. It's a strategy designed to protect your investments by reducing the impact of poor performance in any single investment. When you diversify, you allocate your money across different types of assets, such as stocks, bonds, real estate, and commodities. Within each asset class, you can further diversify by choosing different securities. For instance, in the stock market, you can invest in a mix of industries and companies rather than concentrating all your funds in one particular stock. The rationale behind diversification is to spread risk. Different assets tend to perform differently under various market conditions. For example, when stocks are thriving, bonds may not perform as well, and vice versa. By holding a mix of assets, you aim to balance out potential losses in one area with gains in another, which can help stabilize your overall portfolio returns.

Mutual funds and ETFs are popular tools for achieving diversification without the need for individual stock selection. These investment vehicles provide exposure to a diversified basket of assets, managed by professionals. This way, you benefit from the expertise of fund managers who aim to optimize risk and returns across various market segments.

Diversification is not a guarantee against losses, as all investments carry some level of risk. However, it can be a potent risk mitigation tool, helping investors pursue their financial goals with greater confidence and reducing the chances of severe losses that might result from an over-concentration in a single investment or asset class.

Shifting our focus from diversification, let's explore the riveting world of real-life success stories. These captivating narratives are a testament to the transformative power of financial wisdom and the resilience to overcome challenges, inspiring you on your own path to financial mastery. Prepare to be enthralled by tales of individuals who turned financial aspirations into remarkable achievements, igniting the spark of possibility within you.

Real-Life Success Story: Elon Musk - The Visionary Innovator

Elon Musk, a household name in the world of entrepreneurship and innovation, exemplifies the transformative power of profitable thinking. Musk's journey to financial success began with a deep conviction in his ability to revolutionize industries and change the world.

Diversifying income streams was fundamental to Musk's strategy. While he initially gained recognition through ventures like PayPal, he didn't stop there. He ventured into electric vehicles with Tesla, explored sustainable energy solutions with SolarCity, and set his sights on space exploration with SpaceX. By diversifying across these ambitious ventures, he not only secured financial stability but also positioned himself as a trailblazer in multiple industries.

Career advancement played a pivotal role in Musk's success. His relentless pursuit of knowledge and innovation allowed him to excel in various roles within his companies. He surrounded himself with brilliant minds, forming a professional network that amplified his impact.

Musk's unwavering belief in his ventures and his ability to negotiate complex deals secured him a place among the world's most influential entrepreneurs. When it came to investment vehicles, Musk didn't limit himself to a single realm. He embraced stocks, real estate, and startup investments. His stock holdings in Tesla, for instance, surged in value over time, contributing significantly to his wealth.

Risk management was a cornerstone of Musk's strategy. He understood his risk tolerance and was unafraid of taking calculated risks to achieve his audacious goals. While he faced setbacks along the way, such as SpaceX's initial failures, his resilient mindset allowed him to persevere and ultimately achieve remarkable success.

Elon Musk's story demonstrates that profitable thinking, income diversification, career advancement, and strategic investment choices can pave the way for extraordinary financial success. By following in his footsteps and adopting the psychology of profitable thinking, you too can turn your thoughts into income-generating actions, explore diverse avenues of income, and embark on a journey toward financial abundance.

Chapter 4:

The Psychology of Wealth Building in Business

Building Fortunes, One Mindset at a Time

Crafting Wealth: Exploring the Business Mastery

In this vital chapter, we delve into the art of wealth building within the world of business. The journey to amassing riches is not solely paved with financial strategies and market insights; it's a profound exploration of the human psyche and the power of entrepreneurial mindset. Welcome to 'The Psychology of Wealth Building in Business,' where we unearth the secrets to forging fortunes, one mindset at a time. As we venture deeper into this chapter, you'll discover that wealth creation is not merely about balance sheets and profit margins; it's about fostering the mindset that catalyzes success in the business arena. Join us on this enlightening expedition as we unveil the psychological dynamics that underpin financial triumph and delve into the strategies that turn businesses into wealth-generating powerhouses.

Wealth Mindset

Your mindset in the world of business and wealth-building plays a crucial role in determining your success. This mindset encompasses your beliefs, attitudes, and perceptions related to money, abundance, and financial goals.

At its core, your financial beliefs serve as the bedrock upon which your wealth mindset is constructed. These beliefs often find their roots in the experiences and teachings of your formative years, shaping your outlook on wealth and money matters. They operate as a guiding force, influencing your financial decisions as you navigate the complex landscape of entrepreneurship and business endeavors.

Consider, for instance, the impact of a belief such as "money is the root of all evil." If this notion has taken root in your psyche, it may subtly sabotage your willingness to explore and capitalize on opportunities for wealth-building. On the contrary, those who have been instilled with the belief that "money is a tool for creating a better life" are more likely to proactively seek out and embrace financial opportunities. They view money as a means to achieve their business goals, rather than as a source of apprehension.

Identifying and challenging limiting beliefs within your wealth mindset can be a transformative process. It involves peeling back the layers of your financial psychology to unveil deeply ingrained thought patterns and biases that may be hindering your entrepreneurial journey. By recognizing these barriers, you can gradually replace them with more empowering perspectives on wealth.

In essence, your wealth mindset is not a passive aspect of your business endeavors; it actively shapes your approach to financial opportunities and your capacity to build wealth. It's the lens through which you perceive and interact with the financial world, and its influence extends far beyond mere thoughts – it's the driving force that can propel you toward financial success and prosperity in the business arena.

Abundance vs. Scarcity Mindset

A critical aspect of the wealth mindset is the choice between an abundance mindset and a scarcity mindset. An abundance mindset focuses on the limitless possibilities and opportunities that exist. It views challenges as stepping stones to growth and wealth. In contrast, a scarcity mindset fixates on limitations and fears, often leading to risk aversion and missed opportunities.

Embracing an abundance mindset involves reprogramming your thoughts and beliefs to see abundance in the world, even during challenging times. It encourages you to view your business endeavors as a path to abundance, fostering creativity and innovation.

Money as a Tool

A foundational transformation in embracing a wealth mindset involves reimagining the role of money in your life. Instead of perceiving money as an end in itself, it becomes a powerful tool with which you can achieve your financial goals, both on a personal and business level. This shift in perspective is profound, as it fundamentally alters your approach to wealth accumulation and financial decision-making.

Under a wealth mindset, you begin to view financial decisions not as random or sporadic transactions but as deliberate and strategic choices that align with your long-term vision. Each monetary decision, whether it's investing, saving, or spending, is guided by a thoughtful consideration of how it contributes to your overarching goals. This strategic approach to finances enables you to make choices that optimize resources, minimize risks, and maximize growth.

Money, as your tool, is allocated meticulously to various areas of your life and business. It's no longer seen as an entity to hoard but rather as a resource to be allocated efficiently. Your financial resources are directed towards investments that promise returns, whether it's in the stock market, real estate, or your own entrepreneurial ventures. Moreover, money is utilized to secure valuable resources, whether it's hiring top talent for your business or investing in technology and infrastructure that enhances productivity. Crucially, this perspective on money ensures that every financial decision is deeply aligned with your vision. Whether your goal is to expand your business, support a cause you're passionate about, or ensure financial security for your family, money becomes the means to make those visions tangible. It's no longer about accumulating wealth for its own sake but about utilizing wealth as a vehicle to create the life and impact you desire.

In essence, adopting a wealth mindset is about recognizing that money is a tool in your hands, and how you wield this tool can shape your financial future. This perspective encourages a thoughtful, strategic, and purposeful approach to finances, ensuring that every financial decision is an intentional step toward achieving your dreams and aspirations, both personally and professionally.

Risk Assessment

In the ever-evolving realm of business, risk assessment stands as the indispensable compass that guides organizations through the treacherous waters of uncertainty. It is the strategic process that entails a meticulous evaluation of the potential pitfalls and rewards associated with various choices and actions. By embarking on a journey of comprehensive risk analysis, businesses equip themselves with the insights and foresight necessary to chart a course towards informed, calculated decisions that not only mitigate potential hazards but also pave the way for triumphant success.

Assessing Risks and Rewards: The Keystone of Decision-Making

Effective decision-making in the dynamic and competitive world of business often hinges on the profound ability to assess and harmonize the delicate balance between risks and rewards. Within this intricate balance lies a myriad of choices, each presenting its unique potential benefits and drawbacks. To navigate this complex landscape and make well-informed decisions, it is imperative for businesses to engage in a comprehensive analysis of the risks inherent in each choice they encounter.

These risks are multifaceted, spanning various domains that include the financial, operational, and market-related aspects of the business landscape. In the financial realm, risks may encompass market volatility, currency fluctuations, and credit exposure. Operational risks could manifest as supply chain disruptions, technological challenges, or human resource-related issues. Meanwhile, market-related risks involve factors such as changing consumer preferences, competitive pressures, and regulatory changes.

The essence of effective risk assessment lies in not merely acknowledging the existence of these risks but in gaining a deep understanding of their nature, scope, and potential impact. By embarking on a journey of rigorous risk analysis, businesses empower themselves with the insights required to discern the level of risk associated with each potential decision. This insight, in turn, serves as a guiding beacon, illuminating the path forward with greater clarity and confidence.

A robust risk assessment process equips organizations with the ability to weigh the potential rewards against the identified risks, facilitating a more comprehensive and balanced approach to decision-making. It enables businesses to make informed choices, adapt to changing circumstances, and proactively manage and mitigate potential hazards. Ultimately, effective risk assessment is not just a practical necessity; it is the strategic cornerstone upon which the success and longevity of businesses are built. It empowers organizations to traverse the unpredictable terrain of the business landscape with resilience, adaptability, and a keen eye on the horizon, ensuring that they navigate towards prosperous horizons while effectively steering clear of potential storms.

Cost-Benefit Analysis:

In the intricate realm of risk assessment, the cost-benefit analysis stands as a foundational tool that provides organizations with a clear and structured path to evaluating the potential outcomes of a specific decision or course of action. At its core, this analytical tool involves the quantification and assessment of two critical components: costs and benefits. Costs encompass the financial expenditures an organization anticipates, including both direct and indirect expenses. On the other hand, benefits encompass the anticipated gains and advantages, both direct and indirect, that may result from the decision.

Once costs and benefits are thoroughly quantified, the next crucial step is to balance the equation, weighing the anticipated gains against potential expenditures and drawbacks. This process empowers decision-makers to make choices that are not only well-informed but also strategically aligned with the overarching mission, vision, and goals of the organization.

Advantages of Cost-Benefit Analysis

Conducting a cost-benefit analysis yields several key advantages for organizations. Firstly, it aids in risk mitigation by enabling the identification and proactive management of potential risks associated with a decision. This structured assessment ensures that potential drawbacks and challenges are thoroughly understood and addressed.

Secondly, cost-benefit analysis serves as a mechanism for ensuring that decisions are in harmony with the broader strategic objectives of the organization. It allows decision-makers to assess whether a particular course of action aligns with the mission and long-term goals of the business.

Lastly, and perhaps most importantly, cost-benefit analysis empowers decision-makers to make informed choices based on quantifiable data. Rather than relying on intuition or subjective judgments, organizations can base their decisions on a structured analysis of potential outcomes. This data-driven approach enhances the quality of decision-making and contributes to long-term success and resilience in the ever-changing business environment.

Flexibility and Decision-Making:

In the arena of risk assessment and decision-making, it's crucial to recognize that the outcomes of any decision may be subject to the influence of external factors that lie beyond an organization's control. In this context, flexibility emerges as a vital and indispensable component of the risk assessment process. Businesses must exhibit a nimble and adaptive approach, ever-ready to adjust their strategies in response to emerging information and changing circumstances.

The Importance of Flexibility

Flexibility in decision-making acknowledges the inherent uncertainty of the business landscape. It underscores the need for organizations to remain agile, resilient, and prepared to pivot swiftly in response to unforeseen challenges or unexpected opportunities that may arise. Several key points illuminate the significance of flexibility:

1.**External Factors**: Businesses operate within a dynamic ecosystem influenced by a myriad of external factors, including economic conditions, market trends, regulatory changes, and global events. Flexibility allows organizations to account for these variables and adjust their strategies as necessary to navigate evolving conditions.

2.Risk Management: Flexibility is a fundamental element of effective risk management. It enables organizations to proactively respond to potential risks and mitigate their impact. By remaining adaptable, businesses can implement contingency plans and alternative approaches to address challenges as they arise.

3.Opportunity Recognition: In addition to risk mitigation, flexibility also enhances an organization's ability to seize unexpected opportunities. A flexible mindset encourages proactive exploration of new avenues and the ability to capitalize on emerging trends or market shifts.

4.Enhanced Decision-Making: Flexibility enhances the quality of decision-making by allowing organizations to incorporate new information and insights into their strategies. This adaptability ensures that decisions are well-informed and aligned with current circumstances.

Navigating Uncertainty with Flexibility

In the ever-changing landscape of business, flexibility is the compass that guides organizations through the uncertain terrain. It empowers them to not only manage and mitigate risks effectively but also to harness unforeseen opportunities for growth and innovation.

By cultivating a culture of flexibility and adaptability, businesses position themselves to thrive in an environment characterized by constant change. They are better equipped to make informed decisions, respond to emerging challenges, and leverage evolving trends to their advantage. Ultimately, flexibility is a strategic asset that enables organizations to chart a course towards enduring success and resilience in a world where uncertainty is the only constant.

Behavioral Biases

Behavioral biases are systematic patterns of deviation from rationality in decision-making, often influenced by cognitive shortcuts and emotional factors. The human mind can be influenced by various cognitive biases, which are unconscious mental shortcuts that can lead individuals to make irrational choices. Recognizing and understanding these biases is pivotal in making sound, rational decisions. Let's delve into some of the key behavioral biases:

1. Overconfidence Bias:

Overconfidence bias is a prevalent behavioral bias where individuals tend to overestimate their abilities and underestimate risks associated with a particular decision. This bias can lead to unwarranted optimism and a skewed perception of one's own capabilities. In business, overconfidence can result in taking on projects that are beyond one's capacity or underestimating the challenges involved. To counteract this bias, individuals must engage in self-awareness and critically assess their own skills and limitations. Seeking external feedback and diverse perspectives can help bring a more balanced view into decision-making.

2. Loss Aversion Bias:

Loss aversion bias is a powerful psychological phenomenon where individuals fear losses more than they value equivalent gains. In business, this bias can manifest as a reluctance to embrace potentially beneficial opportunities due to a deep-seated fear of failure. Overcoming loss aversion requires a shift in mindset towards objective risk assessment and calculated risk-taking. It's essential to weigh the potential gains against the potential losses objectively, considering the overall risk-reward profile of a decision.

3. Confirmation Bias:

Confirmation bias involves the tendency to seek out information that aligns with pre-existing beliefs while disregarding or ignoring conflicting evidence. In business decision-making, falling prey to confirmation bias can lead to a skewed perception of reality and reinforce existing opinions. To mitigate confirmation bias, it's crucial to actively seek diverse perspectives, gather a wide range of data, and encourage an open-minded approach. Embracing dissenting viewpoints and challenging preconceived notions can help ensure more balanced and informed decisions.

By acknowledging and addressing these behavioral biases, individuals and organizations can enhance their decision-making processes. The key lies in fostering self-awareness, promoting objective assessment, and actively seeking out diverse perspectives to navigate the behavioral terrain effectively. Ultimately, understanding and mitigating these biases contribute to more rational and well-informed choices in both personal and business

Diversification

Diversification is a fundamental strategy in the realm of wealth building, vital for businesses seeking to bolster financial resilience and stability. At its core, diversification entails spreading investments and income sources across a diverse array of assets and sectors, mitigating risk and avoiding over-reliance on a single source or asset. For businesses, this multifaceted approach goes beyond financial investments and extends to various facets. It involves broadening product offerings to cater to different customer needs, thereby expanding the customer base and reducing reliance on a single product's performance. Geographic diversification comes into play by exploring new markets or regions, each with its unique customer demographics and economic conditions, safeguarding against regional economic fluctuations and capitalizing on growth opportunities. Investment diversification, a critical component, entails allocating financial resources across a spectrum of asset classes, including stocks, bonds, and alternative investments, to minimize the impact of poor-performing assets or market downturns on overall wealth. In essence, diversification is the robust shield against financial uncertainties, fostering stability and long-term prosperity for businesses.

This strategic approach to diversification is pivotal for businesses navigating the ever-evolving landscape of wealth building. It not only safeguards against the inherent risks associated with concentrated investments but also serves as a means to fortify financial foundations. By strategically distributing investments and income sources across a variety of assets and sectors, businesses can withstand economic turbulence and capitalize on opportunities.

Product diversification, one facet of this strategy, empowers businesses to provide a range of products or services that cater to diverse customer needs. This not only expands the customer base but also ensures that success is not solely contingent on the performance of a single product.

Geographic diversification, on the other hand, involves expanding into new markets or regions. By doing so, businesses can tap into different economic conditions and customer demographics, reducing vulnerability to regional economic fluctuations and unlocking the potential for growth in diverse locales.

Investment diversification, a cornerstone of financial stability, entails allocating resources across various asset classes. This includes investments in stocks, bonds, and alternative investment vehicles. Such a diversified investment portfolio mitigates the impact of poor-performing assets or market downturns on overall wealth, enabling businesses to navigate financial challenges with resilience.

In conclusion, diversification is not merely a strategy; it is a fundamental principle that underpins the quest for financial stability and prosperity. For businesses, it represents a comprehensive approach to wealth building, encompassing product diversification, geographic expansion, and prudent investment allocation. Through diversification, businesses not only protect themselves against financial uncertainties but also position themselves for long-term growth and success in an ever-changing business environment.

Real-Life Success Story: Jeff Bezos - The E-Commerce Visionary

Jeff Bezos possessed a wealth mindset that went beyond merely accumulating riches; it was a mindset of relentless innovation and customer-centric thinking. He believed In using wealth as a means to create better experiences and value for customers. Bezos recognized early on that Amazon's success depended on continuously pushing the boundaries of what e-commerce could offer. He didn't view money as an end in itself but as a tool to realize his vision of revolutionizing the way people shop online.

Bezos embraced an abundance mindset. He saw boundless opportunities in the e-commerce landscape and, despite facing challenges, remained focused on growth and innovation. His ability to view challenges as stepping stones and to see the potential for Amazon to expand into various industries showcased his abundance mindset.

For Jeff Bezos, money was a tool to fuel Amazon's expansion and innovation. He strategically allocated resources to enhance customer experiences, invest in new technologies, and diversify

Amazon's product and service offerings. His approach was to leverage wealth as a means to drive the company's mission and long-term success.

Bezos was not risk-averse; instead, he was a calculated risk-taker. When founding Amazon, he recognized the potential of e-commerce, even in the face of skepticism. He conducted thorough risk assessments, understanding that the online retail space was evolving and fraught with uncertainty. However, he saw the immense rewards that could come from being a pioneer in this field. His risk assessment paid off, leading to Amazon's dominance in online shopping.

Jeff Bezos and his team at Amazon consistently applied cost-benefit analysis when expanding into new markets or launching new products. They weighed the potential costs against the benefits, ensuring that each decision aligned with Amazon's long-term strategy. This data-driven approach helped Amazon make informed choices that contributed to its growth.

Throughout Amazon's journey, Bezos exhibited flexibility in response to changing market conditions and emerging opportunities. He pivoted the company from being solely an online bookstore to a diverse e-commerce and technology giant. This adaptability allowed Amazon to stay ahead of competitors and remain relevant in a rapidly evolving business landscape.

Bezos was known for his rational decision-making. He actively sought diverse perspectives and encouraged dissenting viewpoints within Amazon's culture. This approach helped mitigate behavioral biases like overconfidence and confirmation bias, ensuring that decisions were grounded in objective analysis.

Amazon's diversification strategy was exemplified by its expansion beyond e-commerce into cloud computing (Amazon Web Services) and content streaming (Amazon Prime). This diversification shielded

Amazon from over-reliance on a single revenue stream, contributing to its financial stability and resilience.

Embracing the strategies exemplified by Jeff Bezos is not just a path to financial success; it's an invitation to embark on a transformative journey. By adopting a wealth mindset that sees wealth as a tool for positive change, you open doors to innovation and boundless opportunities. Jeff Bezos's story reminds us that an abundance mindset can turn challenges into stepping stones towards growth and prosperity.

Furthermore, using money as a deliberate tool in your entrepreneurial endeavors allows you to strategically shape your financial future. Calculated risk-taking, evidenced by Bezos's Amazon venture, teaches us that well-informed decisions can yield remarkable rewards. Applying cost-benefit analysis ensures that every choice aligns with your overarching mission, while flexibility empowers you to navigate an ever-changing landscape with confidence.

Lastly, fostering a culture of rational decision-making and actively mitigating behavioral biases can lead to more objective, successful outcomes. Jeff Bezos's diversified approach, expanding Amazon's reach beyond e-commerce, demonstrates how businesses can fortify their foundations and thrive in the face of uncertainty.

So, let Jeff Bezos's journey be your inspiration. Embrace these strategies and cultivate your own path to wealth building and entrepreneurial success. The world of business is waiting for your transformative ideas, and the power to forge fortunes truly lies within the grasp of those who dare to dream big, think strategically, and never stop innovating.

Chapter 5:

The Psychology of Innovative Thinking

Igniting Creativity, Fueling Profitability

Unleashing the Inventive Spirit:

In the boundless realm of human creativity, where the seeds of innovation are sown and imagination knows no bounds, lies the captivating journey into "The Psychology of Innovative Thinking." Picture a world where the ordinary transforms into the extraordinary, where problems metamorphose into opportunities, and where the future is shaped by the audacity to question the status quo. Welcome to a chapter that will unravel the enigmatic workings of the human mind, the cradle of innovation itself. As we delve deeper into these pages, prepare to embark on an exhilarating expedition through the intricate labyrinths of innovative thinking. It's a journey that promises to unlock the secrets behind the world's most revolutionary ideas and the minds that conceived them, igniting the spark of innovation within each of us. So, fasten your seatbelts and prepare to traverse the corridors of creativity, for this is where the extraordinary becomes possible, and where innovation knows no bounds.

Open-Mindedness: The Gateway to Innovative Thinking

At the heart of a creative and innovative mindset lies the indispensable trait of open-mindedness. It's a quality that transcends mere receptivity; it's an attitude, a way of approaching the world with a sense of curiosity and an unwavering willingness to embrace the unfamiliar. Open-minded individuals possess a unique capacity to welcome new ideas, diverse perspectives, and unexplored possibilities into their cognitive landscapes. They don't merely accept the status quo or adhere to conventional wisdom; instead, they eagerly traverse uncharted territories in pursuit of innovative solutions.

Open-mindedness represents a liberation from the confines of rigid thinking. It's the audacious act of challenging preconceived notions, biases, and the inertia of tradition. This intellectual flexibility creates fertile ground where innovative thinking can take root and flourish. When people embody open-mindedness, they liberate themselves from the shackles of habitual and linear thinking, opening the door to novel concepts and groundbreaking discoveries.

Crucially, open-mindedness is not a passive state but an active disposition. It encourages individuals to question assumptions, reevaluate paradigms, and entertain the unorthodox. It paves the way for a dynamic and adaptive mindset that can readily pivot in response to changing circumstances. This adaptability is an invaluable asset in the realm of innovative thinking, where the ability to embrace change and navigate new terrain is paramount.

Curiosity: The Engine of Creative Exploration

In the arsenal of the creative mindset, curiosity stands out as a powerful and indispensable tool. It's the spark that ignites the fires of innovation, the insatiable thirst for understanding that propels individuals into uncharted territories of knowledge and possibility. Those who possess a curious disposition are natural inquisitors, driven by an innate desire to ask questions, uncover mysteries, and venture into the realms of the unknown.

Curiosity isn't a mere whim; it's a force that compels individuals to probe deeper, challenge the status quo, and question assumptions. It's the impetus behind that insistent "why" that drives scientific inquiry and the persistent exploration that fuels artistic creativity. Creative thinkers, like intrepid explorers, embark on journeys of discovery, armed with their curiosity as a compass.

One defining characteristic of curious individuals is their childlike approach to problem-solving. They perceive challenges not as daunting obstacles but as intriguing puzzles, beckoning them to unravel their secrets. This perspective infuses the creative process with a sense of wonder and adventure, where each inquiry leads to unexpected connections and each exploration unveils hidden insights.

Moreover, curiosity transcends the boundaries of specific domains of knowledge. It thrives in the fertile grounds of interdisciplinary thinking, where ideas and concepts from diverse fields converge and give birth to innovative solutions. The curious mind is not confined by the limitations of specialization; instead, it revels in the rich tapestry of ideas woven across disciplines.

Unlocking Creativity: The Art of Creative Problem-Solving

In the dynamic realm of innovative thinking and creative problem-solving, a diverse arsenal of creativity techniques emerges as a treasure trove of possibilities. These techniques, akin to the keys that unlock the gates of inspiration, offer structured pathways to navigate the labyrinth of imagination. By wielding these tools, individuals can tap into the boundless reservoir of human creativity, fostering an environment where fresh perspectives and novel solutions flourish.

At its core, the purpose of creativity techniques is to liberate the mind from the shackles of routine thinking and lead it into uncharted territories of innovation. They serve as catalysts for idea generation, transformation, and refinement, elevating the art of problem-solving to new heights.

One fundamental aspect of creativity techniques is their ability to encourage divergence, a process that fans the flames of imagination wide and far. Divergent thinking techniques, such as brainstorming, mind mapping, and the SCAMPER method, promote the generation of a multitude of ideas, unearthing hidden gems from the recesses of the mind. Through these methods, individuals can explore the outer limits of possibility, transcending conventional boundaries to envision innovative solutions.

Equally crucial is the process of convergence, where the scattered fragments of creativity find their way back to form a cohesive, actionable idea. Convergent thinking techniques, such as the Six Thinking Hats and the Delphi method, act as the compass guiding the creative journey. They facilitate the evaluation, selection, and refinement of ideas, ensuring that the most promising concepts are harnessed and developed.

Furthermore, creativity techniques thrive in the fertile soil of collaboration. Group creativity techniques, such as brainwriting and the Nominal Group Technique, harness the collective intellect of teams, allowing a symphony of ideas to harmonize and evolve. In this collaborative arena, the boundaries of individual imagination expand exponentially, giving rise to solutions that transcend the capabilities of a single mind.

Unleashing the Storm: The Art and Science of Brainstorming

In the realm of creativity techniques, few are as celebrated and widely practiced as brainstorming. It stands as a testament to the power of collective thinking, a crucible where ideas are forged and innovation takes flight. Brainstorming is not merely a method; it's a dynamic group activity that invites the unbridled flow of ideas, embracing the notion that creativity knows no bounds.

At its heart, brainstorming is a celebration of quantity over quality, at least in its initial stages. The primary objective is to cast a wide net, capturing a plethora of ideas that span the spectrum of creativity. There are no wrong answers in the world of brainstorming, only stepping stones towards innovative solutions. Participants are encouraged to let their imaginations soar, to challenge conventional thinking, and to explore uncharted territories of possibility.

What makes brainstorming truly remarkable is its collaborative nature. It thrives on the synergy of minds coming together, each adding a unique hue to the canvas of ideas. Within the crucible of a brainstorming session, participants become co-creators, building upon one another's thoughts and insights. It's a process akin to a symphony, where the crescendo of innovation emerges from the harmonious interplay of diverse perspectives.

However, the alchemy of brainstorming is not without its secrets. To harness its full potential, it's imperative to cultivate an environment where creativity can flourish. Trust and psychological safety are the cornerstones upon which brainstorming rests. Participants must feel free to express even the most unconventional ideas without fear of judgment. It is in the embrace of these principles that brainstorming transcends mere technique, becoming a voyage of discovery, and a testament to the limitless power of human imagination.

Mind Mapping

In the labyrinth of innovative thinking, where ideas intermingle and thoughts crisscross, mind mapping emerges as a guiding light, illuminating the non-linear terrain of creativity. This visual creativity technique, akin to an artist's canvas, provides a dynamic space where thoughts and ideas take on a life of their own.

At its core, mind mapping is a method of organizing information that defies the constraints of linear thinking. It's a symphony of interconnected concepts, with the central idea or problem serving as the conductor. Picture a diagram where the nucleus represents your core idea, and from it, branches extend like the limbs of a tree, each branch nurturing a cluster of related thoughts. This hierarchical and associative structure is the essence of mind mapping.

What makes mind maps truly remarkable is their capacity to stimulate associative thinking. Within their sprawling branches and nodes, seemingly unrelated ideas find unexpected connections. It's as if your thoughts are engaged in a lively dance, revealing relationships that might remain hidden in the rigidity of linear thought.

Mind maps shine brightest when it comes to complexity. They excel at unraveling intricate problems or dissecting multifaceted projects. By visually representing the relationships between various elements, mind maps transform complexity into clarity. They serve as a compass, guiding you through the maze of information and illuminating the path forward.

But mind mapping is not merely a tool for organization; it's a catalyst for creativity. As you traverse the branches of your mind map, you'll encounter insights and epiphanies that defy linear thinking. Patterns emerge, connections spark, and innovation takes root. In the world of mind mapping, creativity is not a distant muse but a constant companion.

Stepping into Innovation: Role Play and Simulation

In the vibrant tapestry of creativity, there exists a duo of techniques that beckons individuals to don different hats and step into alternate realities: role play and simulation. These imaginative approaches transcend the boundaries of conventional problem-solving, inviting participants to explore uncharted territories of empathy and alternative perspectives.

Role Play: Empathy in Action

Imagine a stage where participants transform into characters, each intricately woven into the fabric of a complex issue or situation. This is the realm of role play, a creativity technique that fosters a profound understanding of diverse viewpoints. Participants assume various roles or personas related to a problem, embodying them with authenticity and depth. By doing so, they gain an intimate glimpse into the perspectives and motivations of different stakeholders.

Role play is more than a theatrical exercise; it's a gateway to empathetic problem-solving. As participants step into the shoes of others, they break down the walls of preconceived notions and biases. This empathetic exploration often paves the way for innovative solutions that consider the multifaceted dimensions of a challenge. In the world of role play, creativity takes on a human face, and solutions become enriched with understanding and compassion.

Simulations: Learning from Alternate Realities

Now, envision a controlled environment that mirrors the complexities of real-life scenarios. Here, participants engage with this simulated reality to unravel the intricate web of interacting factors and variables. Simulations are the laboratories of creativity, where experimentation reigns supreme without real-world consequences.

Simulations are a dynamic tool employed across various domains, from business and education to healthcare. They offer a platform to test different strategies and scenarios, allowing individuals and teams to grasp the nuances of decision-making in a risk-free setting. This 'learning by doing' approach is a breeding ground for innovative thinking, as it encourages the exploration of alternative paths and the discovery of unexpected outcomes.

These creativity techniques, role play, and simulation, add vibrant colors to the canvas of innovation. They provide structured pathways to stimulate fresh thinking and innovative solutions. While brainstorming fuels idea generation and collaboration, mind mapping encourages associative thinking and visual representation. Role play and simulation, on the other hand, propel individuals into the realms of empathy and scenario exploration.

Incorporating these techniques into the creative process empowers individuals and teams to break free from the shackles of conventional thinking. They encourage participants to step outside their comfort zones, embrace diverse perspectives, and forge innovative solutions to the most intricate and challenging of problems.

The Creative Journey: Unveiling the Creative Process

Creativity, often perceived as an enigmatic force, can be unveiled through a structured and comprehensible process that guides individuals and teams on a transformative journey from inspiration to innovation. This demystification of creativity renders it accessible for a myriad of endeavors, spanning problem-solving, artistic expression, and groundbreaking innovation.

Inspiration: The Spark of Creativity

The inception of the creative process invariably commences with inspiration – that electrifying spark that ignites the flames of imagination. Sources of inspiration are as diverse as the creative minds they kindle, ranging from life experiences and keen observations to challenges and the remarkable creations of others. Inspiration serves as the catalyst propelling individuals to embark on an exploration of novel ideas and innovative solutions.

Ideation: The Blossoming of Ideas

The ideation phase unfolds as the logical progression from inspiration. It is here that a profusion of ideas, intricately connected to the initial spark, is generated. This phase is characterized by divergent thinking, a mindset that encourages the prolific generation of ideas without the immediate imposition of judgment. Techniques such as brainstorming often orchestrate this symphony of creative thought, fostering an environment where the quantity of ideas reigns supreme.

Ideation liberates individuals from the constraints of conventional thinking, beckoning them to traverse the realms of the unconventional and embrace the unbridled freedom of creative ideation. Quantity, in this context, is esteemed over quality, for within the diversity of ideas lies the fertile ground upon which the seeds of innovation are sown.

Implementation: Breathing Life into Creativity

Ideas, however ingenious, remain dormant concepts until they are transmuted into tangible creations, whether they be works of art, innovative solutions, or practical products. The implementation phase is the crucible where the alchemy of creativity occurs. It necessitates meticulous planning, resource organization, and the deliberate execution of steps requisite for the realization of ideas.

For the artist, implementation may encompass the act of painting a canvas, composing a symphony, or penning the pages of a novel. In the realm of business, it could manifest as the development of a groundbreaking product, the orchestration of a strategic marketing campaign, or the implementation of an efficiency-enhancing process.

Implementation signals the transition from divergent thinking, which fueled the generation of ideas, to convergent thinking. This transition entails discernment, decision-making, and the translation of creative vision into practical and actionable steps. The implementation phase often beckons the creative mind to engage in the rigors of problem-solving, experimentation, and the fine-tuning of initial concepts.

Iteration and Refinement: Nurturing Creativity

Innovation and creativity are rarely singular endeavors; they thrive through the embrace of multiple iterations and refinements. The creative journey seldom witnesses the attainment of perfection at its outset. The phase of iteration and refinement stands as a testament to the resilience and adaptability of creators.

This phase not only accommodates but welcomes failure as an inherent and invaluable part of the creative odyssey. Each iteration represents an opportunity for creators to glean insights from missteps, adapt their approaches, and elevate the quality of their creative work. It embodies a commitment to continuous improvement and the relentless pursuit of optimization.

Iteration encourages creators to scrutinize their work with a discerning eye, seeking avenues for enhancement in terms of quality, relevance, and impact. It is a phase that demands patience and unwavering determination, for it may entail setbacks and challenges. However, it is within this crucible of iterative refinement that true innovation flourishes, as creators, fueled by real-world feedback and experiential learning, elevate their ideas and solutions to unprecedented heights.

The creative process, an intricate tapestry interwoven with inspiration and ideation, implementation, and iteration and refinement, is an ever-evolving, dynamic, and cyclical journey. It is a path marked by exploration, experimentation, and evolution. Understanding the distinct stages of the creative process empowers individuals and teams to navigate this expedition more effectively, ultimately leading to the realization of innovative ideas and solutions that have the potential to reshape the world.

Larry Page: Trailblazing the Future - The Open-Minded Curiosity Behind Google's Success

Larry Page, the co-founder of Google and Alphabet Inc., is a prominent figure whose innovative thinking has revolutionized the way we access and interact with information. His entrepreneurial journey exemplifies the principles outlined in "The Psychology of Innovative Thinking."

Larry Page's open-mindedness is evident in his audacious vision to organize the world's information and make it universally accessible. At a time when traditional search engines merely indexed web pages based on keywords, Page and his co-founder, Sergey Brin, developed Google's PageRank algorithm. This revolutionary approach ranked web pages based on their relevance and quality, fundamentally changing the landscape of online search. Page's willingness to challenge the status quo extended to the company's culture. He fostered an environment where employees were encouraged to spend 20% of their work time on side projects, leading to innovations such as Gmail and Google Maps. This open-minded approach not only drove creativity but also expanded Google's offerings beyond search.

Larry Page's insatiable curiosity has been instrumental in Google's success. His fascination with information retrieval and data-driven decision-making led to the development of Google's search engine. Page's curiosity about how search algorithms could be improved, and his desire to understand user behavior, led to continuous innovation in search technology. Furthermore, Page's curiosity extended to moonshot projects through Google X, now part of Alphabet Inc. These projects, including self-driving cars (Waymo) and Project Loon (providing internet access via balloons), showcase his commitment to exploring novel technologies that address global challenges.

Google's success is a testament to the effectiveness of creativity techniques. Larry Page and Sergey Brin used brainstorming and experimentation extensively during Google's early days. They continuously refined their search algorithm, tested new features, and explored innovative revenue models, eventually leading to the company's dominance in the search engine market. Moreover,

Google's commitment to user-centered design and iterative development processes aligns with creativity techniques like iteration and refinement. The company's "launch and iterate" approach allowed them to quickly release products and gather user feedback for continuous improvement, a strategy that has shaped many of Google's services.

Larry Page's innovative journey extends to the creative process, a vital component of his success. His story highlights the significance of each stage, from inspiration to implementation and beyond:

Inspiration: Page's journey began with the inspiration to organize the world's information. This initial spark fueled his relentless pursuit of knowledge and innovative solutions. His curiosity about how search engines worked and the limitations of existing technologies led to the inception of Google.

Ideation: During the ideation phase, Page and Brin generated a multitude of ideas related to improving web search. They adopted a divergent thinking approach, encouraging the generation of numerous concepts without immediate judgment. This prolific generation of ideas ultimately led to the development of the PageRank algorithm, a foundational element of Google's search engine.

Implementation: Larry Page's commitment to turning ideas into reality is evident in Google's transformation from a research project into a global technology giant. The implementation phase involved meticulous planning and resource allocation, as well as the execution of a clear vision. Google's user-friendly interface and efficient search algorithms are a testament to their successful implementation.

Iteration and Refinement: Page's approach embraced iterative refinement, exemplified by Google's continuous improvement of its search algorithm. Feedback from users and ongoing experimentation allowed the company to enhance the quality and relevance of search results. This iterative process contributed to Google's ongoing success and its ability to adapt to changing technology landscapes.

In conclusion, Larry Page's entrepreneurial journey serves as a compelling example of how open-mindedness, curiosity, and adherence to the creative process can lead to groundbreaking innovations. His co-founding of Google, along with his role as Alphabet Inc.'s CEO, showcases the transformative power of innovative thinking. As you embark on your own creative endeavors, take inspiration from Page's story and apply these principles to your pursuit of innovative solutions, whether in technology, business, or any other domain. The path to innovation may be challenging, but it is marked by a continuous commitment to questioning, exploring, and refining ideas to shape a better future.

Chapter 6:

The Psychology of Entrepreneurial Mindsets

Entrepreneurial Thinking for Business Triumph

Navigating the Entrepreneurial Mindset

In the captivating realm of entrepreneurship, where innovation and ambition converge, success is not merely a destination; it's a way of thinking. Welcome to a chapter that delves deep into the very psyche of entrepreneurial triumph. We embark on a voyage to uncover the psychological facets that underpin the entrepreneurial mindset. We'll traverse the terrain of qualities, strategies, and insights that set the stage for triumph in the dynamic world of business. Join us as we explore the mind's labyrinth, where ideas become enterprises, challenges fuel growth, and vision shapes destinies.

Vision: The Guiding Light of Entrepreneurship

Visionary thinking is the cornerstone of the entrepreneurial mindset, illuminating the path to success in the ever-evolving landscape of business. Entrepreneurs, with their audacious ambitions, possess a unique ability to craft a clear and compelling vision of what they aim to accomplish. This vision isn't a mere mirage on the horizon; it's a radiant guiding star that shapes their decisions and fuels their actions.

A well-defined vision is more than a lofty goal; it's a strategic imperative that provides direction, purpose, and a sense of identity. It serves as the answer to fundamental questions that define an entrepreneurial venture, such as "What problem are we solving?" and "What impact do we aspire to make on the world?" This clarity of purpose becomes a North Star, a beacon that not only guides the entrepreneur but also resonates with stakeholders, inspiring teams and aligning their efforts toward a common and noble goal.

Yet, visionary thinking transcends the realm of abstraction; it is a dynamic process of transformation. Entrepreneurs possess the remarkable ability to distill their grand vision into actionable steps, meticulously crafting strategies, plans, and objectives that bridge the chasm between aspiration and execution. This translation of dreams into a pragmatic roadmap is where the alchemy of entrepreneurship truly unfolds.

Moreover, the power of vision lies in its resilience and unwavering persistence. It serves as the compass that keeps entrepreneurs on course, even when they navigate turbulent waters of challenges and uncertainties. It is the source of their unyielding determination, the fuel that propels them forward despite setbacks. In the face of adversity, the entrepreneurial vision remains unshaken, motivating teams and stakeholders alike, reminding them of the greater purpose that propels the journey.

In the entrepreneurial world, vision is not a mere concept; it's the life force that transforms dreams into reality, shapes industries, and leaves an indelible mark on the world. It's the essence of entrepreneurial spirit, and its luminous glow beckons innovators to explore uncharted territories, create lasting change, and leave a profound legacy.

The Anatomy of Entrepreneurial Vision

A visionary entrepreneur's journey is not just about having grand aspirations; it's about meticulously crafting a roadmap that transforms dreams into tangible achievements. Let's delve deeper into the essential components of entrepreneurial vision:

1. Clarity of Purpose: At the heart of any powerful vision lies a crystal-clear understanding of the problem being solved or the opportunity being seized. Entrepreneurs keenly identify the pain points of their target audience, envisioning a future where these issues are alleviated or transformed. This clarity serves as the foundation upon which the entire venture is built.

2. Inspiration and Motivation: An entrepreneurial vision isn't just a destination; it's a wellspring of inspiration and motivation. Entrepreneurs draw upon their vision to inspire themselves and others. It becomes a rallying cry that ignites passion, fosters commitment, and propels teams forward, even when faced with adversity.

3. Alignment and Focus: In the complex landscape of business, an entrepreneurial vision acts as a guiding compass, helping entrepreneurs navigate through a sea of possibilities. It assists in aligning resources, efforts, and strategies toward a singular, overarching goal. This focus is vital for efficient resource allocation and effective decision-making.

4. Flexibility and Adaptability: While a visionary entrepreneur holds steadfast to the core of their vision, they also possess the wisdom to adapt and pivot when necessary. The entrepreneurial journey is often riddled with unexpected twists and turns. Visionaries embrace change and are willing to adjust their strategies while keeping their ultimate destination in sight.

5. Communication: An entrepreneurial vision is not a well-kept secret but a story that must be eloquently told. Entrepreneurs excel in articulating their vision, making it resonate with stakeholders, investors, customers, and employees. Effective communication fosters buy-in and support, galvanizing everyone involved to work cohesively toward the shared goal.

6. Continuous Improvement: Visionary thinking is not a one-time act but an ongoing process. Entrepreneurs constantly refine and enhance their vision as they gain insights, learn from experiences, and adapt to changing market conditions. This commitment to continuous improvement ensures that the vision remains relevant and impactful.

7. Impact and Legacy: Beyond mere financial success, visionary entrepreneurs seek to make a lasting impact on the world. Their vision extends beyond profit margins to encompass social, environmental, or cultural change. They aspire to leave a legacy that inspires future generations of innovators.

In the entrepreneurial realm, a well-crafted vision is not a passive concept but a dynamic force that propels individuals and teams toward exceptional achievements. It embodies the spirit of audacity, innovation, and unwavering determination, setting visionary entrepreneurs apart on their remarkable journeys of creation and transformation. As we journey further into the realm of the entrepreneurial mindset, we shall uncover more layers of the entrepreneurial psyche that contribute to their extraordinary success.

Resilience: Rising Strong in the Face of Adversity

Resilience is an indomitable hallmark of the entrepreneurial mindset. It embodies the ability to not only weather the storms of adversity but to emerge from them stronger and more determined than ever before. In the tumultuous landscape of entrepreneurship, where uncertainty and challenges abound, resilience is the bedrock upon which success is built. Navigating obstacles as opportunities, resilient individuals possess a unique perspective. Rather than perceiving setbacks as insurmountable barriers, they view them as invaluable opportunities for growth and learning. Every failure and setback become a stepping stone on the path to success, transforming adversity into advantage.

A Positive Outlook and Unwavering Commitment

Learning from failure is a key facet; resilient entrepreneurs not only embrace failure but actively seek its lessons, understanding that within the ashes of failure lie the seeds of future success. Positivity sustains them; maintaining a positive attitude in the face of adversity is a defining trait of resilience. Resilient entrepreneurs cultivate a mindset that remains unshaken, even when confronted with daunting challenges, knowing that optimism fuels perseverance. Their commitment amidst uncertainty is unwavering; resilience is the unwavering commitment to long-term objectives, even in the midst of unpredictability. Anchored by a sense of purpose that transcends the turbulence of the present, they stay steadfast in their pursuit of their vision. Prioritizing self-care is also integral; resilient entrepreneurs recognize the importance of maintaining physical and mental well-being through strategies like mindfulness, regular exercise, and seeking support from mentors or peers. In the entrepreneurial arena, resilience is the cornerstone that upholds the vision and fortitude of individuals and teams. It is the unwavering belief that in the face of adversity, there is an opportunity to rise stronger, learn more, and achieve greater heights.

Grit and Determination: The Unwavering Drive

Grit, often likened to the fusion of passion and unwavering perseverance, stands as another integral facet of the entrepreneurial mindset. Entrepreneurs who embody grit are characterized by their relentless determination to reach their goals, undeterred by the formidable challenges or setbacks that might cross their path.

At its core, grit signifies a profound and enduring commitment to their endeavors. These individuals understand that the journey of entrepreneurship demands substantial dedication and effort, and they are willing to invest the hard work required to surmount the inevitable obstacles that arise. Grit is synonymous with a profound sense of purpose, a burning desire that propels them forward, even when the attainment of success appears distant or elusive.

A defining trait of grit is the capacity to sustain motivation across extended durations. Entrepreneurs possessing grit do not readily capitulate when confronted with adversity; instead, they perceive setbacks as mere temporary roadblocks along the inexorable path to success. This unwavering determination, bordering on tenacity, consistently distinguishes them throughout their entrepreneurial odyssey.

The journey of an entrepreneur often mirrors a rollercoaster ride, filled with unpredictable twists and turns. It's during these tumultuous moments that grit shines the brightest. Gritty entrepreneurs possess an innate ability to weather storms and emerge stronger from the tempests of uncertainty.

Grit isn't just about resilience; it's about resilience with an unyielding resolve to persevere. When faced with financial setbacks, market turbulence, or even the naysayers who doubt their vision, entrepreneurs with grit stand unwavering. They refuse to let circumstances define their destiny.

Moreover, gritty entrepreneurs lead by example. Their determination becomes a source of inspiration for their teams and a rallying point for their supporters. It's this infectious spirit that galvanizes others to join in the pursuit of a shared dream. Through their actions, gritty entrepreneurs foster a culture of perseverance and tenacity, creating teams and organizations that thrive in the face of adversity.

In the annals of entrepreneurship, success stories are replete with instances where grit proved to be the differentiator. It's the entrepreneur who tirelessly pitched their idea to countless investors before securing funding. It's the startup founder who faced rejection after rejection but continued refining their product until it captured the market's imagination. These stories are testament to the formidable force that is grit, propelling individuals to defy the odds and transform their visions into reality.

Networking and Relationship Building

Entrepreneurial success isn't solely predicated on groundbreaking ideas or impeccable execution; it's also profoundly influenced by the art of networking and relationship building. In the labyrinthine world of business, these skills transcend mere social interactions; they are deeply intertwined with the human psyche.

At its core, networking is the conscious act of fostering connections and nurturing relationships that extend far beyond the exchange of business cards or digital connections. It delves into the fundamental human need for social interaction and affiliation. This psychological underpinning is crucial for understanding why networking holds immense significance in entrepreneurship.

From a psychological standpoint, networking fulfills our innate desire to belong to a community or tribe. It provides a sense of identity and belonging, which, when experienced in a professional context, can be profoundly fulfilling. Entrepreneurs who actively engage in networking are essentially responding to this deep-seated psychological need for connection and validation.

Furthermore, the psychology of networking is intertwined with the principle of reciprocity, a fundamental aspect of human behavior. Entrepreneurs who invest time and effort in building relationships and offering value to others are tapping into this psychological phenomenon. When they extend a helping hand or provide support to their network, it triggers a psychological inclination in their connections to reciprocate. This reciprocity manifests in various forms, from valuable advice and support to collaborative ventures and lucrative business opportunities. Entrepreneurs who grasp and leverage this psychological principle effectively often find themselves at the nexus of a web of mutually beneficial relationships.

Building relationships in the entrepreneurial realm transcends the transactional nature of conventional networking. It's about creating a complex web of trust, credibility, and shared purpose. These connections evolve into an invaluable source of emotional support, encouragement, and validation, all of which are essential for maintaining mental and emotional well-being on the tumultuous entrepreneurial journey.

In essence, entrepreneurial networking isn't just about expanding one's professional circle; it's a multifaceted psychological and emotional exchange. It not only satisfies our fundamental human needs for connection and reciprocity but also fuels our ambitions and aspirations. It's the delicate dance of human psychology and business acumen that renders networking a potent force in the entrepreneurial toolkit.

Mentorship and Guidance

In the entrepreneurial landscape, the quest for mentorship and guidance is akin to a psychological beacon guiding aspirants through the labyrinth of uncertainty and challenges. This practice transcends the mere exchange of knowledge; it taps into profound psychological mechanisms that underpin personal growth and success.

At its core, mentorship is a manifestation of our innate human inclination to seek guidance and wisdom from those who have walked the path before us. This psychological predisposition is deeply rooted in our evolutionary history, where learning from experienced individuals within a tribe or community was paramount for survival. In the contemporary entrepreneurial context, this instinctual drive translates into a fervent quest for mentors who can illuminate the path to success.

From a psychological perspective, mentorship operates as a mechanism for accelerated learning and personal development. Entrepreneurs who seek mentors are essentially leveraging a cognitive shortcut – learning from the mistakes and successes of others. This practice aligns with the psychological principle of heuristic decision-making, where individuals rely on mental shortcuts to make efficient choices. In this case, entrepreneurs are bypassing the arduous trial-and-error process by gleaning insights from the experiences of their mentors.

Moreover, mentorship satisfies our intrinsic need for affiliation and belonging. The mentor-mentee relationship often transcends the purely professional realm, evolving into a deep bond of trust and shared aspirations. This psychological connection contributes to a sense of emotional support and security, vital for maintaining mental and emotional well-being in the face of entrepreneurial challenges.

The psychological dynamics of mentorship also intertwine with the concept of self-efficacy – one's belief in their ability to achieve goals and overcome challenges. Through mentorship, entrepreneurs receive not only knowledge but also a potent dose of encouragement and validation. This psychological boost bolsters their self-confidence, empowering them to take on audacious challenges and persist in the face of adversity.

The Role of Trust in Mentorship

One of the central psychological components of mentorship is trust. Trust forms the bedrock of mentor-mentee relationships and is pivotal in facilitating knowledge transfer and personal growth. From a psychological standpoint, trust is a multifaceted concept with deep implications for the mentorship dynamic.

Trust in mentorship is a manifestation of psychological safety. When entrepreneurs seek mentors, they are essentially entrusting their dreams, aspirations, and vulnerabilities to another individual. This requires a profound sense of psychological safety, wherein the mentee believes that their mentor has their best interests at heart and will provide guidance without judgment.

The psychological principle of reciprocity also plays a significant role in mentorship. Entrepreneurs often trust their mentors because they believe that their commitment to the relationship will be reciprocated with valuable insights and support. This reciprocal expectation fosters a sense of fairness and psychological equilibrium in the mentorship dynamic.

Furthermore, trust in mentorship aligns with the psychological concept of social identity theory. When entrepreneurs form mentor-mentee relationships, they often identify with their mentors and their mentors' successes. This psychological identification not only strengthens the mentorship bond but also instills a sense of belonging and shared identity.

From a cognitive perspective, trust simplifies information processing. Entrepreneurs are more receptive to mentorship when they trust their mentors, as trust reduces cognitive barriers to accepting advice and guidance. This psychological phenomenon is rooted in the human tendency to favor information that aligns with preexisting beliefs and values, known as confirmation bias. In mentorship, trust can counteract confirmation bias, allowing mentees to consider alternative perspectives and insights.

Bootstrapping: Navigating Entrepreneurship on a Shoestring

Bootstrapping, in the context of entrepreneurship, refers to the practice of building and growing a business with minimal external financial resources, often relying on personal savings, revenue generated by the business itself, and sweat equity. Bootstrapped businesses aim to become financially self-sufficient and sustainable without seeking significant external funding, such as venture capital or loans.

Key Characteristics

1.**Minimal External Financing**: Bootstrapped businesses prioritize using their own funds, generated revenue, and available resources to fund their operations and growth. They aim to minimize reliance on external investors or loans.

2.Sustainable Growth: Bootstrapping focuses on achieving steady, sustainable growth rather than rapid expansion. This approach allows businesses to maintain control and avoid excessive debt.

3.Efficiency and Resourcefulness: Bootstrapped entrepreneurs are resourceful and efficient, often finding creative solutions to challenges and making the most of available resources.

4.Risk Management: Bootstrapping minimizes financial risk by avoiding significant debt or equity investments. Entrepreneurs take calculated risks and maintain financial control.

Bootstrapping Strategies

1.Self-Funding: Entrepreneurs use their personal savings or assets to fund the initial stages of the business. This can include investing personal money, selling assets, or utilizing retirement savings.

2.Revenue Generation: Bootstrapped businesses prioritize generating revenue from their products or services as quickly as possible. This revenue is reinvested into the business to fuel further growth.

3.Lean Operations: Bootstrappers are known for running lean operations, minimizing unnecessary expenses, and focusing on essentials. This includes keeping a close eye on overhead costs and avoiding unnecessary hires.

4.Sweat Equity: Entrepreneurs often contribute their time, skills, and labor to the business without drawing a significant salary initially. This "sweat equity" is seen as an investment in the business's future success.

5.Profit Reinvestment: Instead of distributing profits to investors, bootstrapped businesses reinvest profits back into the company to finance expansion, product development, or marketing efforts.

Mark Zuckerberg: A Real-Life Inspiration of Vision and Resilience

Mark Zuckerberg, the co-founder and CEO of Facebook (now Meta Platforms, Inc.), provides an inspiring real-life illustration that aligns with several key principles discussed in this chapter. His journey serves as a compelling testament to the importance of vision, resilience, grit, networking, and mentorship in the world of entrepreneurship.

Mark Zuckerberg's journey commenced with a clear and audacious vision. In 2004, while still a college student at Harvard, he envisioned a global social networking platform that would redefine how people connect and share information. His vision transcended the ordinary; it aimed to revolutionize the way individuals interacted with one another. This vision was the propellant for the creation of Facebook.

In the face of adversity and numerous obstacles, Facebook remained resilient. Legal challenges, technical hurdles, and fierce competition from other social networking sites could have deterred a less determined team. However, Mark Zuckerberg and his colleagues exhibited unwavering commitment and determination. They viewed challenges not as roadblocks but as stepping stones, each setback an opportunity for growth and improvement.

Networking played a pivotal role in Facebook's rapid ascent. Mark Zuckerberg recognized the power of the network effect, where users' invitations to friends exponentially expanded the platform's reach. This viral growth was a testament to the importance of fostering connections and leveraging social dynamics for success.

Furthermore, Zuckerberg actively sought mentorship and guidance. He understood the value of learning from those with more experience. For instance, Sean Parker, the co-founder of Napster and an early advisor to Facebook, provided invaluable insights and mentorship during Facebook's formative years. This mentorship helped Zuckerberg navigate the complexities of the tech industry and make informed decisions.

Mark Zuckerberg's journey, from a college dorm room to creating one of the world's largest social media platforms, embodies the entrepreneurial mindset. His resolute commitment to his vision, resilience in the face of adversity, ability to harness the power of networking, and openness to mentorship all played pivotal roles in his success.

Mark Zuckerberg's remarkable journey isn't limited to just those in the business world; it resonates with anyone striving for personal growth and success in their chosen endeavors. His example underscores the universal principles of visionary thinking, resilience, determination, and the value of networking and mentorship. Whether you're an aspiring entrepreneur, an artist, an academic, or pursuing any other passion, Mark Zuckerberg's story offers valuable insights on how to navigate challenges, pursue your vision, and build meaningful connections that can enrich your life and career. His journey encourages individuals from all walks of life to embrace their goals, overcome obstacles, and continually seek opportunities for growth and impact.

Chapter 7:

The Psychology of Decision-Making in Business

Sculpting Success through Strategic Minds

Decoding Business Decision-Making

Welcome to the captivating realm of decision-making in the dynamic landscape of business. As we embark on this journey through the intricate web of choices and strategies, we'll uncover the psychology that underpins every pivotal decision. Decision-making isn't merely a series of logical calculations; it's an intricate dance of human cognition, emotions, and intuition. In this chapter, we'll unravel the mysteries behind why we make the choices we do in the business world and how gaining insight into these psychological factors can be the key to sculpting success. Get ready to explore the minds of strategic thinkers and discover the art of making decisions that can shape the destiny of companies and careers alike.

Rational Decision-Making

Rational decision-making stands as the cornerstone of sound business choices, underpinning a structured and systematic approach that has guided countless successful endeavors. At its core, this approach represents a meticulous process of evaluating options, assessing risks, and predicting outcomes to arrive at the most logical and optimal decision possible.

In theory, rational decision-making assumes a world where individuals possess complete and accurate information, enabling them to make choices that invariably maximize their utility or align with their objectives. It presumes a decision-maker who adheres to a consistent and rational decision-making process, devoid of the influences of emotions or irrationality.

The rational decision-making process unfolds in several distinct steps, each contributing to a comprehensive and well-informed choice. It commences with the identification of the problem or decision at hand, setting the stage for a focused examination of the issue. This initial step is crucial, as it defines the scope and nature of the decision, creating a clear roadmap for what follows.

The next pivotal phase involves the systematic gathering of relevant information. Decision-makers cast a wide net to collect data, facts, and insights that are pertinent to the issue. This step is akin to assembling the pieces of a complex puzzle, where each fragment contributes to a completer and more accurate picture.

With data in hand, the decision-maker moves on to the critical task of evaluating available alternatives. This phase demands a comprehensive analysis of the options at one's disposal. It requires careful consideration of the potential benefits, drawbacks, and implications associated with each alternative. It's a cerebral exercise where objectivity and a data-driven mindset take center stage.

Simultaneously, the consequences of each alternative are scrutinized. What ripple effects might each choice trigger? How do these align with the desired outcomes? These are the questions that permeate this stage of the process. It's a forward-looking perspective that aims to anticipate the ramifications of each decision path.

The ultimate culmination of the rational decision-making model is the selection of the option that best aligns with the desired outcome. This choice isn't a product of intuition or gut feeling; it's a calculated selection, grounded in the meticulous analysis of available data and the logical assessment of alternatives.

However, it's important to acknowledge the chasm between theory and practice. In the real world, complete and flawless information is often a mirage. Decision-makers grapple with imperfect data, cognitive biases, and time constraints that can hinder the pursuit of fully rational choices. Nevertheless, the rational decision-making model serves as a guiding light, offering a structured framework for systematic decision-making in the complex terrain of business.

Behavioral Economics

Behavioral economics, a fascinating intersection of psychology and economics, ushers us into a realm where human decision-making transcends the confines of traditional rationality. This field of study acknowledges the complexities of the human mind and how emotions, cognitive biases, and social influences intermingle to shape choices in economic and business contexts.

At its core, behavioral economics challenges the conventional notion of Homo economicus, the rational decision-maker who consistently maximizes utility. Instead, it dives into the intricacies of human behavior, recognizing that individuals often deviate from the pristine paths of rationality.

One of the fundamental concepts explored in behavioral economics is bounded rationality. This notion posits that decision-makers operate within the constraints of limited cognitive resources. In the real world, people often face information overload and time constraints that preclude exhaustive analysis. To cope, they employ heuristics or mental shortcuts, simplifying complex decisions into more manageable processes. This adaptive strategy allows individuals to navigate the complexities of decision-making efficiently.

Another captivating phenomenon illuminated by behavioral economics is prospect theory. This theory challenges the traditional economic assumption that individuals weigh potential gains and losses equally. Instead, it reveals a fascinating asymmetry in human behavior. When confronted with the prospect of gains, individuals tend to be risk-averse, preferring the certainty of smaller gains over the allure of larger but uncertain ones. Conversely, when faced with potential losses, they often become more risk-tolerant, seeking to avoid losses at all costs, even if it involves taking greater risks.

The implications of behavioral economics ripple across the business landscape, offering profound insights into consumer behavior and employee motivation. By delving into the intricacies of human decision-making, businesses can refine their marketing strategies, optimize product design, and develop more effective employee engagement techniques.

Understanding the psychological underpinnings of consumer choices allows businesses to tailor their marketing efforts to resonate with the emotional and cognitive triggers that drive purchasing decisions. Likewise, recognizing the impact of bounded rationality on employee decision-making empowers organizations to design incentive structures and workplace environments that promote better choices and enhance overall performance.

Ethical Decision-Making

Ethical decision-making stands as a moral compass guiding individuals and organizations through the intricate landscapes of business. At its core, it involves the art of discerning right from wrong when confronted with complex ethical dilemmas. These dilemmas, often the crucible of ethical decision-making, emerge when conflicting moral principles or values cast a shadow over the path forward, leaving decision-makers grappling with profound choices.

In the realm of business, ethical dilemmas manifest in diverse contexts, each presenting a unique set of moral intricacies. Product safety, a critical concern for consumers, compels businesses to balance profitability with the well-being of their customers. Employee treatment shines a spotlight on issues of fairness, respect, and social responsibility within the workplace. Environmental impact raises questions about sustainability, resource utilization, and the long-term health of our planet. Financial practices, a domain where temptation and ethical lapses can surface, challenge businesses to maintain transparency and integrity.

Navigating these ethical quagmires requires more than mere intuition; it necessitates a structured approach that carefully considers the moral implications of each choice. Ethical decision-makers embark on a journey of thoughtful reflection, weighing the potential consequences of their actions on a multitude of stakeholders. They ponder the far-reaching ripples of their choices, from customers and employees to the broader community and the environment.

Central to ethical decision-making is the unwavering commitment to making choices that align with ethical principles and values. This commitment transcends the allure of short-term gains or expediency and holds fast to the principles that underpin trust, credibility, and social responsibility.

Moreover, ethical decision-making is not a solitary endeavor but often a collective effort, involving input and perspectives from diverse stakeholders. Engaging in open dialogue and seeking the counsel of ethics committees or advisors can shed light on blind spots and offer a more comprehensive understanding of the moral terrain.

Stakeholder Consideration

Stakeholder consideration lies at the heart of ethical decision-making within the intricate framework of business ethics. In this complex landscape, where moral principles and financial interests intersect, the welfare and interests of all stakeholders become paramount. A stakeholder, in essence, is anyone who can be affected, either directly or indirectly, by an organization's actions and decisions. This inclusive group encompasses employees, customers, suppliers, shareholders, the surrounding community, regulatory bodies, and beyond.

The essence of ethical decision-making in business involves recognizing and honoring the diverse needs, expectations, and rights of these stakeholders. It necessitates a holistic approach that transcends mere profit-maximization and embraces the principles of fairness, justice, and social responsibility.

Consider a scenario where a company grapples with an ethical dilemma related to product safety. In this scenario, the decision-makers must meticulously weigh the interests of multiple stakeholders. Customers, as the end-users of the product, rightly expect safety and reliability. Their well-being and trust are on the line. Employees, who may be intimately involved in the production process, also have a stake in the quality and safety of the products they create. Their concerns about product integrity and workplace ethics are legitimate. Shareholders, who have invested in the company with an eye on profitability, seek financial returns. Balancing these divergent interests while upholding ethical principles becomes the ethical imperative.

Ethical decisions in such cases strive to navigate a path that respects the rights and well-being of all stakeholders involved. It seeks to harmonize competing interests while adhering to ethical principles and societal norms. This intricate balancing act is not merely about making everyone happy; rather, it is about ensuring that no stakeholder is unjustly harmed or disadvantaged by the decisions made.

The concept of stakeholder consideration extends beyond individual decisions and permeates the broader corporate culture. It entails fostering a corporate environment that values transparency, accountability, and open communication with stakeholders. Ethical organizations actively seek feedback, engage in stakeholder consultations, and embrace mechanisms for reporting ethical concerns. They recognize that the long-term success and reputation of a company are intimately tied to its relationships with stakeholders.

Furthermore, stakeholder consideration is closely intertwined with the psychological concept of empathy. Decision-makers who possess empathy can better understand and appreciate the perspectives and needs of various stakeholders. This heightened awareness enables them to make decisions that reflect a deeper understanding of the human impact of their choices.

In an era where ethical considerations significantly influence consumer preferences and investor decisions, stakeholder consideration emerges as a cornerstone of sustainable and responsible business practices. Ethical decision-makers who champion stakeholder interests are not only sculpting success in their organizations but also fostering a legacy of trust, social responsibility, and enduring ethical excellence.

Group Decision-Making

Group decision-making, a critical facet of business decision processes, delves into the intricate web of interactions, influences, and dynamics that unfold within decision-making groups. The outcomes of group decisions can shape the trajectory of an organization, making it essential to understand and optimize the dynamics at play.

At the core of effective group decision-making lie the dynamics of how individuals within the group interact. These dynamics encompass a multitude of elements, each contributing to the overall process and outcome:

1.Communication Patterns: Effective group dynamics hinge on open, clear, and respectful communication. Research shows that teams that communicate openly and transparently are 50% more likely to make informed decisions. Members must express their thoughts, ideas, and concerns candidly while actively listening to others. Encouraging a culture of open dialogue fosters the exchange of diverse perspectives and information crucial for informed decisions.

2.Power Dynamics: Within any group, power dynamics inevitably emerge. These dynamics may be formal, such as hierarchical authority, or informal, where certain individuals wield influence based on expertise, charisma, or personality. Understanding and managing these power dynamics is crucial to ensure that decisions are not dominated by a select few but are representative of the group's collective wisdom.

3.Roles and Responsibilities: In decision-making groups, individuals often assume different roles based on their skills, expertise, or personalities. These roles can range from leaders and facilitators to critics and synthesizers. Research has found that when roles are clearly defined and distributed effectively, group performance can improve by up to 30%.

Groupthink

It's a psychological occurrence wherein cohesive groups prioritize consensus and conformity over critical evaluation and independent thinking when making decisions. This tendency to seek harmony and avoid conflict can lead to suboptimal or even disastrous choices.

The dynamics of groupthink can manifest in several ways. First, there's the illusion of invulnerability, where group members may develop an inflated sense of confidence, believing that their decisions are infallible. This can lead to reckless risk-taking. Then comes collective rationalization, where in the pursuit of consensus, group members may collectively downplay or rationalize away potential issues or challenges associated with their decisions. Often, there's the belief in inherent morality, where groupthink involves the belief that the group's decisions are inherently moral or righteous, leading members to ignore ethical or moral concerns.

Stereotyping outsiders is another facet; outsiders or dissenting individuals may be stereotyped as the enemy or as uninformed, stifling diverse perspectives. Self-censorship is common, with group members censoring themselves, refraining from voicing dissenting opinions or concerns to maintain group harmony. The illusion of unanimity is another peril; silence is misconstrued as agreement, leading to a false perception of unanimous support for a decision. Finally, there's direct pressure on dissenters: those who do voice dissenting opinions may face direct pressure or even coercion to conform to the group's views.

The consequences of groupthink can be severe, leading to decisions that are poorly thought out, high-risk, or ethically problematic. Examples from history, such as the Challenger space shuttle disaster and the Bay of Pigs invasion, underscore the dangers of groupthink in critical decision-making contexts.

Preventing groupthink necessitates a conscious effort to foster an environment where diverse viewpoints are not only welcomed but actively encouraged. Effective group leaders play a crucial role in this process by promoting a culture of constructive debate and dissent. Strategies to mitigate groupthink include appointing a designated devil's advocate within the group to challenge prevailing assumptions and arguments, creating a safe space where individuals feel comfortable expressing dissenting opinions without fear of retribution, consulting with external experts or seeking input from individuals outside the group to introduce fresh perspectives, allowing group members to provide feedback anonymously, and changing the group leader periodically to prevent the entrenchment of a single perspective.

Decision-Making Tools

Decision-making tools are indispensable aids in both the business arena and everyday life. These versatile instruments encompass techniques like scenario planning and decision trees, serving as structured methodologies to dissect choices, evaluate outcomes, and arrive at well-informed decisions. By harnessing these tools, individuals and organizations can elevate the caliber of their decision-making, mitigate risks, and capitalize on opportunities. Whether tackling intricate business challenges or navigating personal life decisions, these tools offer clarity and direction, guaranteeing that choices align harmoniously with goals and aspirations.

Decision Trees

Decision Trees are powerful visual tools that offer decision-makers a structured and intuitive approach to analyze complex choices. These trees serve as a roadmap for navigating decision options and potential outcomes by breaking them down into a series of interconnected choices and their corresponding consequences.

Picture a decision tree as a branching flowchart, where each decision node represents a choice to be made, and each branch signifies a possible outcome or consequence of that choice. These visual representations help decision-makers gain a comprehensive understanding of the different paths they can take and the potential results associated with each decision.

Decision trees find their greatest utility in decisions characterized by multiple variables and uncertainties. When confronted with intricate choices involving various factors, these visual aids simplify the decision-making process by providing clarity and structure.

For instance, consider a scenario where a company is contemplating the launch of a new product. Such a decision entails considering numerous variables like market demand, production costs, and the competitive landscape. In this context, a decision tree becomes invaluable. It allows decision-makers to visually map out the potential consequences of different choices. By evaluating these outcomes, individuals and organizations can make more informed and strategic decisions.

The flexibility and adaptability of decision trees make them a versatile tool applicable across diverse domains. From financial planning to project management and from healthcare diagnostics to environmental impact assessments, decision trees serve as a valuable asset in dissecting intricate decisions. Their visual nature not only enhances comprehension but also facilitates effective communication among team members and stakeholders.

Scenario Planning

Scenario planning, a powerful strategic decision-making tool, unfolds as an essential practice in the ever-evolving landscape of business and beyond. Acknowledging the inherent uncertainty of the future, this approach empowers decision-makers to navigate the labyrinth of possibilities with foresight and agility.

Scenario planning's core principle involves crafting a spectrum of plausible future scenarios, each representing a distinct narrative of what the future might hold. These scenarios encompass a broad array of variables, including economic conditions, technological advancements, market trends, and geopolitical shifts. By meticulously delineating these scenarios, organizations gain a multifaceted lens through which they can anticipate and prepare for a spectrum of potential futures.

Imagine a global corporation, its operations spanning continents and industries. In the face of an unpredictable world, such an entity harnesses scenario planning to fortify its resilience. It envisions scenarios that span from geopolitical upheavals and market disruptions to natural calamities. Each scenario becomes a narrative thread, guiding the organization's strategy in the face of diverse, plausible futures.

The potency of scenario planning lies in its capacity to transcend the confines of linear thinking. It shatters the limitations of single-track strategies, acknowledging that the future is a complex tapestry woven from myriad threads of uncertainty. In adopting this methodology, organizations not only prepare for what they expect but also for what might surprise them—a trait indispensable in today's dynamic landscape.

Moreover, scenario planning engenders adaptability. Armed with insights from multiple scenarios, decision-makers are poised to pivot and recalibrate their strategies as circumstances evolve. Rather than being caught off guard, they are primed to seize opportunities and mitigate risks in an ever-shifting environment.

These decision-making tools—decision trees, and scenario planning—provide structured approaches to analyzing and evaluating choices. They assist decision-makers in assessing complex situations, quantifying impacts, and preparing for an uncertain future. By leveraging these tools, individuals and organizations can make more informed and strategic decisions in various business contexts.

The Path to Innovation: Bill Gates' Inspiring Journey in Technology and Business

In the ever-evolving realm of technology and business, few individuals have left as indelible a mark as Bill Gates. His journey from a computer whiz kid to co-founding one of the world's most influential technology companies, Microsoft, serves as an inspiring testament to the power of vision, determination, and innovation.

Gates embarked on his entrepreneurial journey at a young age, displaying an insatiable curiosity and an innate talent for programming. Together with his childhood friend Paul Allen, he saw a future where personal computers would become an integral part of everyday life. Their vision was audacious - to place a computer in every home and on every desk. This vision laid the foundation for what would become Microsoft.

In the early days, Gates faced numerous challenges. He navigated a rapidly evolving technology landscape, fierce competition, and the daunting task of developing software for a nascent industry. Yet, in the face of adversity, he exhibited unwavering determination and resilience. Gates and his team viewed each obstacle as an opportunity for growth and innovation.

Networking played a pivotal role in Microsoft's ascent. Gates recognized the power of partnerships and collaborations. His strategic alliance with IBM to provide an operating system for their first personal computer catapulted Microsoft into the limelight. This moves not only solidified Microsoft's position but also paved the way for personal computing to become a household phenomenon.

Furthermore, Gates actively sought mentorship and guidance. He understood the value of learning from those with more experience. His interactions with industry giants like Steve Jobs and Warren Buffett provided invaluable insights and mentorship during Microsoft's formative years. This mentorship helped Gates navigate the complexities of the tech industry and make informed decisions.

Bill Gates' journey, from a young computer enthusiast to co-founding one of the world's leading technology companies, embodies the entrepreneurial mindset. His unwavering commitment to his vision, resilience in the face of adversity, ability to harness the power of networking, and openness to mentorship all played pivotal roles in his success.

But what makes Bill Gates' story truly remarkable is that it transcends the realm of business. It resonates with anyone striving for personal growth and impact in their chosen endeavors. His example underscores the universal principles of visionary thinking, resilience, determination, and the value of networking and mentorship.

Whether you're an aspiring entrepreneur, or simply someone passionate about making a difference, Bill Gates' journey offers valuable insights. It demonstrates how to navigate challenges, pursue audacious visions, and build meaningful connections that can enrich your life and career. Bill Gates is not just an icon in the tech world; he is a beacon of inspiration for anyone with a dream and the determination to turn that dream into reality.

Thanks to your dedication and interest, I'm thrilled to present these gifted sections for you all. Beyond the inspiring stories and wisdom, we've uncovered, there are treasures waiting to be explored

In the spirit of continuous growth and learning, let's not halt our journey here. Beyond the inspiring stories and wisdom, we've uncovered, there are gifted sections waiting to be explored. These sections are repositories of knowledge and insights, holding the potential to expand our horizons and fuel our aspirations.

GIFTED

SECTION :1

The Psychology of Leadership for Profit

Leading Toward Prosperity and Beyond

Leadership Styles

Leadership style profoundly influences how leaders interact with their teams and, in turn, the impact on organizational profitability. Understanding different leadership styles is essential for leaders to choose the most suitable approach for achieving their profit goals.

Transformational leadership is a style that focuses on inspiring and motivating team members to achieve exceptional results. Leaders who adopt this style often lead by example and encourage innovation and creativity among their teams. By instilling a shared vision and enthusiasm, transformational leaders can drive increased productivity and, ultimately, higher profitability.

Transactional leadership, on the other hand, is characterized by clear structures and defined expectations. Leaders in this category use rewards and punishments to motivate their teams. They emphasize efficiency and compliance, which can be effective in certain situations but may not foster the same level of innovation and long-term profitability as transformational leadership.

Servant leadership is rooted in the idea that leaders serve their teams rather than vice versa. They prioritize the well-being and growth of their team members. This approach builds trust and loyalty, resulting in enhanced team cohesion and job satisfaction. In turn, satisfied and motivated employees are more likely to contribute positively to the bottom line.

Emotional Intelligence

Emotional intelligence (EQ) is a critical component of effective leadership. Leaders with high EQ possess the ability to recognize and manage their own emotions and those of others. This skill is particularly important in leadership roles, as it influences decision-making, team dynamics, and ultimately, organizational profitability.

Leaders with high EQ are better equipped to navigate the complex world of interpersonal relationships. They can effectively communicate with team members, address conflicts, and build strong rapport, all of which contribute to a harmonious work environment. Such an environment is more likely to yield higher employee morale and productivity, both of which are crucial for profitability.

Additionally, leaders with strong EQ are often skilled in empathizing with their team members' experiences and challenges. This empathy fosters trust and mutual respect. When employees feel understood and valued, they tend to be more engaged and committed, driving higher performance levels that directly impact profitability.

Adaptive Leadership

Adaptive leadership is a dynamic approach that focuses on leading through change and uncertainty, skills that are increasingly vital in today's rapidly evolving business landscape. Leaders who embrace adaptive leadership practices are better equipped to guide their organizations through challenges and seize opportunities for profit.

Adaptive leaders possess the ability to diagnose the situation and determine the most appropriate leadership style and strategies based on the context. They are not bound to a single leadership approach but are flexible and responsive to the needs of their teams and organizations. This adaptability enables them to lead effectively in various scenarios, whether it's a period of growth, crisis, or transformation.

Furthermore, adaptive leaders encourage a culture of learning and experimentation. They understand that innovation and adaptability are closely linked to profitability. By fostering an environment where employees are encouraged to learn, experiment, and adapt to changing circumstances, adaptive leaders can drive a culture of continuous improvement and innovation that positively impacts the bottom line.

Effective Communication

Effective communication lies at the heart of successful leadership. It involves the clear and efficient exchange of information, ideas, and feedback between leaders and team members, as well as among team members themselves. In the context of leadership for profit, effective communication plays a pivotal role in achieving organizational goals.

Leaders must master several facets of effective communication:

1.**Active Listening**: Effective leaders are active listeners. They pay close attention to what team members are saying, seeking to understand their perspectives, concerns, and ideas fully. Active listening fosters trust and makes team members feel valued, ultimately enhancing collaboration and productivity.

2.**Clear Messaging**: Leaders must convey their messages clearly and concisely. Ambiguity and misunderstanding can lead to costly mistakes or inefficiencies. Clear communication ensures that everyone understands expectations, goals, and the path to profitability.

3.Non-Verbal Communication: It's not just what leaders say but also how they say it. Non-verbal cues, such as body language, facial expressions, and tone of voice, can convey confidence, sincerity, and empathy. Leaders who align their non-verbal communication with their verbal messages are more likely to influence positively.

Influence and Persuasion

Leaders often need to influence and persuade others to achieve specific objectives, whether it's convincing team members to adopt a new strategy or persuading stakeholders to support an important project. Effective influence and persuasion can have a direct impact on profitability.

Ethical Influence: Ethical leaders use their influence to encourage behaviors and decisions that align with organizational values and goals. They avoid manipulative tactics and instead rely on transparency, credibility, and trust.

Building Credibility: Credibility is essential for effective influence. Leaders who consistently demonstrate expertise, integrity, and reliability earn the trust of their teams and stakeholders. Credibility makes it easier to persuade others to follow a particular course of action.

Negotiation Skills: Negotiation is a core leadership skill, especially in situations involving profitability. Leaders must be adept at finding mutually beneficial solutions and reaching agreements that advance organizational interests.

Effective communication and influence go hand in hand. Leaders who communicate clearly and persuasively can align their teams and stakeholders toward profit-oriented objectives. They can articulate a compelling vision, address concerns, and inspire commitment, ultimately driving profitability.

Moreover, by mastering the art of ethical influence, leaders can build stronger relationships with team members and stakeholders, fostering a collaborative atmosphere that supports the pursuit of profit while maintaining trust and integrity.

Corporate Social Responsibility (CSR) Strategies

CSR involves the integration of social and environmental concerns into business operations. Leaders who embrace CSR recognize that it goes beyond philanthropy; it is a strategic approach that can have a direct impact on profitability.

Brand Differentiation: Companies that engage in CSR activities often stand out in a crowded market. Consumers increasingly support businesses that are socially responsible. A strong CSR strategy can differentiate a brand, attract socially conscious customers, and lead to increased market share and profitability.

Risk Mitigation: CSR strategies address risks related to environmental and social issues. Proactively managing these risks can prevent costly incidents, regulatory fines, and reputation damage. Risk mitigation contributes to financial stability and long-term profitability.

Innovation and Efficiency: CSR initiatives often drive innovation and efficiency. Sustainability practices can lead to cost savings through reduced energy consumption, waste reduction, and resource optimization. These efficiencies positively impact profitability by improving the bottom line.

Sustainability Leadership

Sustainability leadership involves a commitment to environmental stewardship and responsible resource management. Leaders who champion sustainability recognize that it is not only an ethical imperative but also a driver of profitability.

Resource Efficiency: Sustainability leaders prioritize resource efficiency in their organizations. This includes minimizing waste, reducing energy consumption, and optimizing supply chain operations. Resource-efficient practices can lower operational costs, directly impacting profitability.

Market Opportunities: Sustainability initiatives can open new market opportunities. Consumers increasingly seek products and services that align with their values. By offering sustainable options, organizations can tap into growing market segments and increase revenue streams.

Long-Term Planning: Sustainability leaders take a long-term view of their organizations. They understand that responsible resource management and environmental practices contribute to resilience and longevity. Long-term planning protects profitability by ensuring the organization's continued success in a changing world.

In summary, leading with ethics and corporate social responsibility is not only the right thing to do but also a strategic approach that can drive profitability. Ethical leadership fosters trust, employee morale, and legal compliance. CSR strategies differentiate brands, mitigate risks, and drive innovation and efficiency. Sustainability leadership promotes resource efficiency, market opportunities, and long-term planning, all of which directly impact the bottom line.

GIFTED

SECTION:2

The Psychology of Persuasion

Unlocking Minds, Influencing Choices

Customer Needs Analysis

Understanding and catering to customer needs are fundamental in sales. Successful sales professionals begin by conducting a thorough customer needs analysis. This involves more than just identifying what the customer wants; it's about comprehending their motivations, challenges, and aspirations.

To conduct a customer needs analysis effectively, salespeople need to ask probing questions and actively listen to the customer's responses. This process helps uncover pain points, desires, and specific requirements. For instance, in the context of selling business software, a needs analysis might reveal that a customer is looking for a solution to streamline their invoicing process and reduce administrative overhead.

Once these needs are identified, sales professionals can tailor their sales pitch and product recommendations to directly address these pain points and deliver clear value to the customer. Understanding customer needs not only boosts the likelihood of making a sale but also builds trust and rapport.

Buying Motivations

Every customer has distinct buying motivations. These motivations are the driving forces that lead someone to make a purchasing decision. They can vary widely from one individual to another and from one product or service to another.

Common buying motivations include solving a problem or pain point, fulfilling a desire or aspiration, achieving financial savings, gaining social status, or simply enjoying a pleasurable experience. For example, a customer buying a high-end sports car may be motivated by the desire for prestige and the thrill of speed, while another customer purchasing a fuel-efficient hybrid car may be motivated by cost savings and environmental consciousness.

Sales professionals who understand these motivations can align their sales approach and messaging to resonate with the customer's specific buying drivers. It's about speaking directly to what matters most to the individual, making the sales pitch highly relevant and persuasive.

Emotional Triggers

Emotions play a significant role in decision-making. Customers often make buying decisions based on how a product or service makes them feel. Emotions such as excitement, fear, joy, trust, or a sense of belonging can strongly influence purchasing choices.

Identifying and appealing to these emotional triggers is a key aspect of effective salesmanship. For instance, a travel agency might tap into a customer's desire for adventure and exploration when promoting exotic vacation packages. By using evocative language and imagery, they can stimulate the customer's emotions and create a sense of anticipation.

Moreover, the emotional aspect of sales extends to the salesperson's demeanor and communication style. Sales professionals who convey genuine enthusiasm, empathy, and confidence can establish an emotional connection with customers, making them more receptive to the sales message.

Trustworthiness and Credibility

Building trust is foundational in sales. Trust is the bedrock upon which lasting customer relationships are built. Trustworthy sales professionals are perceived as credible, reliable, and honest. To establish trustworthiness, it's essential to:

Demonstrate Expertise: Customers trust those who exhibit expertise in their field. Sales professionals should have a deep understanding of their products or services, industry trends, and customer pain points. Sharing this knowledge builds confidence in the salesperson's ability to provide valuable solutions.

Transparency: Honesty and transparency are crucial. Salespeople should be forthright about the benefits and limitations of their products or services. This builds credibility and reassures customers that they are making informed decisions.

Consistency: Consistency in actions and messaging reinforces trust. When salespeople consistently deliver on promises and maintain integrity, customers are more likely to trust their recommendations.

Active Listening

Active listening is a vital skill in building rapport and understanding customer needs. It involves genuinely paying attention to what the customer is saying, without interrupting or prematurely formulating responses. Active listening includes:

1.**Empathetic Listening**: Sales professionals should seek to understand not only the words but also the emotions and concerns underlying what the customer is expressing. Empathy fosters a sense of being heard and understood.

2.**Asking Clarifying Questions**: To ensure a comprehensive understanding, salespeople should ask clarifying questions to dig deeper into the customer's needs and challenges. This demonstrates genuine interest in addressing their specific requirements.

3.Paraphrasing and Summarizing: Repeating and summarizing what the customer has shared helps confirm understanding and shows that the salesperson values their perspective.

Empathy and Connection

Building rapport relies on creating a personal connection with the customer. This connection goes beyond the transactional aspect of the sale and is grounded in empathy and genuine interest in the customer's well-being. Key elements include:

1.Empathy: Empathy involves recognizing and understanding the customer's emotions and perspectives. When customers feel that the salesperson truly cares about their concerns, a stronger connection is formed.

2.1Building Rapport: Building rapport is about finding common ground or shared interests with the customer. It could be a shared hobby, a similar background, or a mutual connection. These commonalities help create a sense of camaraderie.

3.Customized Interaction: Sales professionals should aim to tailor their interactions to each customer's preferences and communication style. Some customers prefer a formal approach, while others appreciate a more relaxed and friendly demeanor.

Consultative Selling

Consultative selling is an approach where sales professionals act as trusted advisors to their customers. Instead of merely pushing products or services, they engage in meaningful conversations to understand customer needs and offer tailored solutions. Key components include:

1.Needs Assessment: Salespeople start by asking questions and conducting thorough needs assessments to identify customer pain points and goals.

2.Solution Presentation: Based on the needs assessment, sales professionals present solutions that directly address the customer's specific challenges, providing a clear value proposition.

3.Educational Approach: Consultative sellers educate customers about the features, benefits, and long-term value of their offerings. They aim to empower customers to make informed decisions.

Handling Objections

Handling objections is a critical sales skill. Objections can arise for various reasons, including concerns about price, timing, or perceived risks. Effective techniques for addressing objections include:

Active Listening: Sales professionals should actively listen to the customer's objection, allowing them to fully express their concerns before responding.

Empathetic Responses: Empathy is essential in objection handling. Acknowledge the customer's concerns and express understanding.

Providing Solutions: Address objections by presenting solutions or counterarguments that alleviate the customer's concerns. This might involve offering additional information, testimonials, or options that mitigate perceived risks.

Psychological Persuasion Principles

Effective persuasion in sales often relies on well-established psychological principles. Understanding and applying these principles can significantly enhance a sales professional's ability to influence buying decisions. Key principles include:

Scarcity: The principle of scarcity suggests that people tend to desire things more when they believe they are scarce or in limited supply. Sales professionals can use scarcity by highlighting limited-time offers, low stock availability, or exclusive promotions to create a sense of urgency.

Social Proof: Social proof is the idea that people are more likely to follow the actions of others, especially when they are uncertain about a decision. Salespeople can leverage this by showcasing customer testimonials, reviews, or endorsements from trusted figures.

Reciprocity: The principle of reciprocity suggests that when someone receives something valuable, they feel compelled to give something in return. Sales professionals can offer free resources, trials, or samples to potential customers, creating a sense of obligation to reciprocate by making a purchase.

The Psychology of Financial Wellness

Unlocking Financial Wellness: The Mindset Matters

Taking Control of Your Financial Future

In this enlightening section, we embark on a transformative journey into the realm of personal finance management, a vital skill that transcends career choices and applies to every individual seeking financial security and fulfillment in life. While business endeavors may not be your primary pursuit, the knowledge and mastery of personal finance are universal cornerstones that can pave the way for a more secure and enriching future. Join us as we delve into the intricacies of financial empowerment, equipping you with the tools to shape your destiny through sound financial practices and mindful decision-making.

The Basics of Financial Literacy

Your personal finances are like an intricate puzzle, where each piece meticulously fits into the larger picture of your financial well-being. This multifaceted puzzle encompasses various components, encompassing how you earn, spend, save, and invest your money. In this extensive and illuminating exploration, we will delve deep into each fragment of this financial puzzle, providing you with profound insights into how they interconnect and profoundly shape your financial landscape.

By acquiring a profound comprehension of these fundamental aspects of financial literacy, you'll empower yourself to make informed, strategic decisions that will not only fortify your financial security but also catapult you toward achieving your most ambitious life and financial objectives. Join us on this enlightening odyssey into the realm of financial literacy, where you will unveil the keys to mastering your personal finances and seizing control of your financial destiny.

Budgeting: Crafting Your Financial Roadmap for Success

Picture the process of creating a budget as if you were meticulously sketching out a well-thought-out plan for your financial journey. In this comprehensive and illuminating exploration, we will unravel the intricate art of budgeting, a skill that serves as your guiding compass in the complex world of personal finance.

A budget empowers you to allocate your hard-earned income with precision and foresight. It acts as your financial GPS, ensuring that you're adeptly balancing essential expenditures while simultaneously earmarking resources for your loftiest goals and aspirations. As we navigate through the depths of budgeting, you will gain profound insights into the strategies and techniques that will not only bolster your financial security but also pave the way for realizing your most audacious life and financial dreams.

Embark on this enlightening voyage into the realm of budgeting, where you will acquire the tools and knowledge to sculpt your financial destiny according to your terms. Whether your goals involve achieving financial independence, buying a dream home, or traveling the world, a well-crafted budget is your first-class ticket to success.

Saving for the Future

The act of saving money transcends the mere establishment of a financial safety net; it is the art of bestowing upon oneself a myriad of possibilities. Through the disciplined and consistent practice of saving, individuals embark on a journey that not only fortifies them against unforeseen emergencies but also paves the way for addressing forthcoming expenses and seizing serendipitous opportunities.

In this enlightening and expansive exploration, we will delve deep into the profound significance of saving for the future. It is a financial endeavor that extends far beyond the boundaries of simple thriftiness; it is a calculated and strategic act that empowers individuals to take control of their financial destinies.

Discover the transformative potential of saving consistently, as we navigate through the intricacies of allocating your financial resources with purpose and foresight. Explore the various facets of saving, from establishing emergency funds that provide a robust buffer against the unexpected, to earmarking resources for upcoming financial obligations and even positioning yourself to grasp unforeseen prospects.

The Power of Informed Financial Decisions

The power of Informed financial decisions lies at the heart of achieving financial success and security. While the concept of decision-making may seem mundane, its ramifications are profound, shaping the trajectory of one's financial life. Whether you are a seasoned investor or just starting to chart your financial course, the art of making informed financial decisions is a skill of paramount importance.

At its core, informed financial decision-making involves a thoughtful and deliberate process of evaluating choices, weighing risks and rewards, and aligning your financial actions with your long-term goals. It's a proactive approach to managing your financial resources that goes beyond simply reacting to financial circumstances.

One of the fundamental pillars of informed financial decisions is budgeting. Creating a well-structured budget allows you to track your income and expenses, providing clarity on where your money goes. This foundational step helps you allocate funds to your essential needs, savings, and investments, ensuring that your financial house is in order.

Investing is another key aspect of informed financial decisions. It involves understanding various investment vehicles, risk tolerance, and time horizons. By making informed choices about where to invest your money, you can harness the power of compounding, allowing your wealth to grow over time. Diversification, asset allocation, and periodic portfolio reviews are essential elements of effective investment decision-making.

Moreover, informed financial decisions extend to managing debt wisely. It's about understanding the types of debt you hold, their interest rates, and crafting a strategy to pay them off efficiently. By doing so, you can reduce financial stress and free up resources for other financial goals.

Financial literacy is the bedrock upon which informed financial decisions are built. It empowers you to understand complex financial concepts, decipher investment jargon, and navigate the intricacies of the financial world. Armed with knowledge, you can make choices that align with your values and aspirations.

Informed financial decisions are not made in isolation. They are influenced by your unique financial goals, risk tolerance, and life circumstances. Therefore, it's crucial to periodically review and adjust your financial decisions as your life evolves.

Investing: Growing Your Money

Investing is a multifaceted art that involves the strategic allocation of financial resources with the aim of generating returns and building wealth over time. This chapter delves into the expansive world of investing, underscoring its paramount importance in personal finance and the accumulation of wealth.

To embark on a journey of informed investment decisions, it's imperative to acquaint oneself with the diverse landscape of investment vehicles. These vehicles encompass a wide array, including but not limited to stocks, bonds, mutual funds, exchange-traded funds (ETFs), real estate, and more. Each investment type boasts its distinct characteristics, risk-reward profiles, and suitability for an array of financial objectives.

Risk inherently intertwines with investing, and comprehending the risk-return dynamics is fundamental. Diverse investment types carry varying degrees of risk; stocks, for instance, often tantalize with the promise of higher potential returns but come hand in hand with greater volatility. Conversely, bonds tend to offer a more stable investment but may yield comparatively lower returns. It's the judicious blending of these assets within a diversified investment portfolio that acts as a shield, mitigating risk while simultaneously seeking an equilibrium between potential returns and safeguarding one's financial interests.

The temporal dimension of investing, represented by your investment time horizon, wields significant influence over your investment strategy. Short-term financial objectives may necessitate the adoption of a more conservative investment approach, safeguarding capital in the process. However, long-term goals provide the luxury of embracing a more aggressive strategy that actively seeks higher returns over an extended period. For example, retirement accounts are characterized by their extended time horizons, allowing investors to harness the exponential power of compounding.

The pivotal compass guiding your investment journey is your set of well-defined investment goals. Identifying the raison d'être of your investments is quintessential. Whether your focus is on securing a comfortable retirement, funding a future home purchase, or financing your child's education, these goals chart the course for your investment choices and strategies. The pursuit of long-term objectives may prompt a diversified approach, encompassing a blend of equities (stocks) and fixed-income investments (bonds), while shorter-term aspirations might necessitate a concentration on low-risk, liquid assets like certificates of deposit (CDs) or money market accounts.

In the intricate tapestry of investment management, the twin concepts of diversification and asset allocation form the bedrock of risk mitigation and wealth optimization. Diversification unfolds as a prudent risk management technique, with the principle of spreading investments across different asset classes and geographic regions. This diversification strategy cushions the potential impact of underperforming investments on your overall portfolio. Asset allocation, on the other hand, pertains to the strategic distribution of your investments among these different asset classes, aiming to strike an optimal balance between risk and return.

Navigating the realm of investment accounts is essential for an astute investor. Understanding the nuances of various accounts, such as individual retirement accounts (IRAs), 401(k)s, brokerage accounts, and more, is crucial. Each type of account comes imbued with unique tax advantages, regulations, and implications that significantly influence your investment decisions and tax liabilities.

Lastly, an arsenal of investment strategies awaits the discerning investor. These strategies span a spectrum that includes value investing, growth investing, dividend investing, and passive investing, which entails the use of ETFs or index funds. Each strategy adheres to distinct principles and objectives, aligning with specific risk tolerances, financial goals, and investment horizons.

Financial Wellness: A Journey, Not a Destination

Financial wellness is an ongoing journey, a path of continuous decision-making that significantly impacts your financial future. Unlike a fixed destination, it's a dynamic process that evolves with each choice you make. Personal finance management transcends mere numbers; it's about the daily decisions and actions that mold your financial well-being over time.

Imagine your financial wellness journey as a road trip, with each financial choice resembling a pit stop along the way. These decisions include budgeting, saving, investing, and spending. They also involve more nuanced choices, such as how you prioritize financial goals, manage debt, and handle unexpected expenses.

Every choice you make has consequences that ripple through your financial life. For instance, diligently saving a portion of your income today can lead to a comfortable retirement in the future. Conversely, overspending or neglecting to budget can create financial stress down the road.

Financial wellness is not a one-size-fits-all concept; it's tailored to your unique circumstances and aspirations. Your journey may include milestones like paying off debt, building an emergency fund, or achieving specific financial goals. Along the way, you'll face challenges, temptations, and unexpected detours that require adaptability and resilience.

Crucially, financial wellness is not a fixed state; it's fluid and adaptable. Life circumstances change, financial goals evolve, and economic conditions fluctuate. Your ability to navigate these shifts and make informed decisions is at the core of financial wellness.

Mastering the Art of Financial Wellness

"Mastering the Art of Financial Wellness" is a transformative journey that goes beyond numbers and budgets, delving deep into the intricate world of personal finance. In this comprehensive guide, you will explore the principles and practices that lead to a secure and prosperous financial future. From smart spending and consumer awareness to building a sturdy financial foundation and overcoming challenges, this chapter equips you with the tools to navigate the complexities of your financial journey with wisdom and confidence.

Smart Spending and Consumer Awareness

Imagine being a savvy shopper who makes well-informed choices. By being mindful of your spending and understanding consumer tactics, you can get more value from your hard-earned money. Smart spending is not just about finding deals and discounts; it's about aligning your purchases with your priorities and values. Consumer awareness empowers you to question advertising claims, compare prices, and resist impulse buying. It's a fundamental aspect of financial wellness, helping you maximize the utility of every dollar you spend.

Balancing Present Enjoyment with Future Goals

Imagine walking on a tightrope between enjoying today and planning for tomorrow. Striking a balance between treating yourself now and securing your future is a key aspect of financial wellness. It involves setting financial goals that reflect your aspirations, whether it's buying a home, traveling the world, or retiring comfortably. By finding this equilibrium, you ensure that your financial decisions support both your immediate pleasures and your long-term dreams.

Building a Strong Foundation for Life

Just as a solid foundation supports a building, understanding personal finance creates a sturdy base for your life's journey. It's about establishing a financial framework that can withstand life's uncertainties and fluctuations. A strong foundation encompasses various aspects of financial wellness, from budgeting and saving to investing and protecting your assets. It provides stability, peace of mind, and the flexibility to pursue your life goals.

Emergency Funds: Your Safety Net

Imagine an umbrella on a rainy day – that's what an emergency fund provides. It's a buffer that safeguards you from unexpected financial storms. Building and maintaining an emergency fund is a vital component of financial wellness. It ensures that you have the resources to cover unforeseen expenses, such as medical bills, car repairs, or job loss, without resorting to high-interest debt. It offers financial security and peace of mind, allowing you to navigate life's challenges with confidence.

The Value of Financial Education

Knowledge is a valuable tool. By seeking financial education and being open to learning, you can make better decisions and set yourself up for long-term success. Financial education is not limited to formal courses; it encompasses a continuous process of self-improvement. It involves staying informed about financial trends, understanding investment options, and honing your money management skills. Embracing the value of financial education empowers you to take control of your financial future.

Strengthening Financial Habits

Think of financial habits as the building blocks of your financial foundation. Small, consistent actions can lead to significant results over time. Whether it's developing a habit of saving a portion of your income, paying bills on time to maintain a good credit score, or regularly reviewing your financial goals, these habits shape your financial well-being. Strengthening positive financial habits ensures that you are continually working toward your financial objectives.

Automating Savings and Investments

Imagine setting up a system that automatically saves and invests a portion of your income. This approach eliminates the temptation to spend money impulsively and ensures that you're consistently working toward your goals. Automating your finances simplifies the process of wealth-building. It allows you to allocate a portion of your income toward savings and investments before you have a chance to spend it. This disciplined approach fosters financial growth and helps you reach your financial milestones more efficiently.

Tracking Your Finances

Picture yourself as a detective unraveling the mysteries of your spending patterns. Tracking your expenses gives you a clear picture of where your money is going and helps you identify areas where you can cut back or make adjustments. It's like shining a spotlight on your financial habits, illuminating areas of strength and areas that may need improvement. By regularly monitoring your finances, you gain valuable insights into your spending behaviors and can make informed decisions to align your financial choices with your goals.

Overcoming Financial Challenges

Financial challenges are part of life, but your mindset and strategies can make a difference. Dealing with Debt Strategically Imagine chipping away at a mountain one stone at a time. Paying off debt requires a strategic approach, prioritizing higher-interest debts and working towards becoming debt-free. It's a journey that demands discipline and determination, but the rewards are financial freedom and reduced stress.

Adapting to Changes and Setbacks

Life is full of unexpected twists and turns. Building resilience means being prepared to adapt to changes, whether they're job-related, health-related, or economic. It involves creating a financial safety net that can weather unexpected setbacks, such as medical emergencies, job loss, or economic downturns. Resilience empowers you to bounce back from adversity and continue your financial journey.

Seeking Financial Advice and Resources

While you may not be pursuing a business path, seeking advice from financial professionals can be immensely beneficial. Financial Advisors: Your Personal Guides Think of financial advisors as navigators on your financial journey. They can help you create a comprehensive plan, offer insights, and guide you towards your financial goals. Collaborating with experts can provide you with a deeper understanding of complex financial concepts, personalized strategies, and access to resources that enhance your financial wellness journey.

I want to extend my heartfelt gratitude to each of you. Your dedication to learning and growth has been the driving force behind this exploration into the intricate realms of business and personal finance. Your trust and commitment inspire me every day. I would like to take a moment to express my sincere appreciation for allowing me to be your guide on this enlightening journey. Your thirst for knowledge and your unwavering curiosity are testaments to your determination to succeed in the ever-evolving world of finance and entrepreneurship. As we part ways for now, I leave you with a profound thought: In the world of business and finance, the quest for knowledge is unending. Stay vigilant and always be open to new ideas, strategies, and opportunities. Remember, the path to success is illuminated by the light of continuous learning.

Until we meet again in the future, whether in the pages of this book or beyond, I wish you boundless success, unwavering prosperity, and a future filled with exciting possibilities.

-GAURAV BAGHEL

www.ingramcontent.com/pod-product-compliance
Lightning Source LLC
Chambersburg PA
CBHW062321290526
45794CB00005B/1850